YOUR LIFE YOUR WAY

LIVE YOUR DREAM LIFE

Milind Sahasrabudhe

INDIA • SINGAPORE • MALAYSIA

Notion Press

No.8, 3rd Cross Street,
CIT Colony, Mylapore,
Chennai, Tamil Nadu – 600004

First Published by Notion Press 2020
Copyright © Milind Sahasrabudhe 2020
All Rights Reserved.

ISBN 978-1-63669-726-0

This book has been published with all efforts taken to make the material error-free after the consent of the author. However, the author and the publisher do not assume and hereby disclaim any liability to any party for any loss, damage, or disruption caused by errors or omissions, whether such errors or omissions result from negligence, accident, or any other cause.

While every effort has been made to avoid any mistake or omission, this publication is being sold on the condition and understanding that neither the author nor the publishers or printers would be liable in any manner to any person by reason of any mistake or omission in this publication or for any action taken or omitted to be taken or advice rendered or accepted on the basis of this work. For any defect in printing or binding the publishers will be liable only to replace the defective copy by another copy of this work then available.

Contents

Introduction 5

PART 1 – Passion

* Evolution of 'Job' concept * 9
* What is Passion? * 13
#MissionPassion™ 23
Convert your passion into Career 28
* Passion to Success Story of Raj * 43
Some Final Thoughts 56
Summary 59

PART 2 – 5 Secret Principles of Wealth

When Sam met Hari 63
5 Secret Principles of Wealth 67
Sam grows the Business 102
Venturing into a Niche 104
Building a Health Hub 111
Bid Goodbye! 115
Summary 120

List of priceless Books 123
My other books in the 'Money-Minds' series 124

Introduction

We as human beings have all the emotions like any other animal. The only distinguishing characteristic of human is the ability 'to think'. We are social animal too and prefer to stay in groups or communities. We help each other to improve our lives. Humans invented many things that helped to make life better. To support our community life, we invented concept of sharing of work as per the skills that in turn helped to discover concept of factories, jobs and Money. In the initial days, humans were treating them just a medium to 'Earn a Living'. But, over time, these external things have become so dominant that our entire life is just revolving around them. We cannot think or act beyond a job, money etc. Most of us are just 'Earning a Living' and have forgotten to 'Live'.

Many of us are simply working day by day, month by month, year by year just to 'Earn a Living'. They work in a job or a business because they are earning money and having a good lifestyle. Agree, that they are having a 'great lifestyle'. But do they have a 'great Life'? I doubt. You may say, don't we have to work to earn money. Yes, of course, we have to. What I am saying is you must always remember that career, job or money are external things and they are created by humans and we need to consider them as byproduct of our work that we love to do and are good at. We call this as 'Passion'. If we work on what we love, chances of success are high. Living by doing what you love is a 'Life worth Living'.

In first part of this book, I am going to discuss, why it is important to 'do what you love'. I have tried to explain how one can find his/her passion and how that passion can be converted into a career to lead a happy life.

In second part of the book, I have tried to explain, 'How one can create great wealth with a career or business based on his/her passion by following 5 secret principles. I strongly believe that, finding and working on the passion is important but what is equally important is, creating a value and wealth based on that passion (monetizing your Passion). Principles mentioned here are simple, easy to implement yet effective. These principles are based on my study of successful people, so they are time tasted and proven.

My commitment is to make 1 crore (10 million) Money-Minds who have a better understanding of money and would work to add value with their passion rather than just following the money. I am sure, you will build a Successful career with your passion and create wealth beyond your wildest dreams. Live, 'Your Life, Your Way'

– Milind
India's First Money-Minds Coach

PART 1

Passion

* Evolution of 'Job' concept *

Our ability to question the things around us had led to many inventions and humans have developed socialized communities.

Humans created social life and developed rules to live in the society. To run these societies and improve lives of the people we developed many things. These things were used to be created by different families in ancient days. For e.g., farmers used to grow crops, mason used to create houses, cobblers used to create footwear and so on.

These people used 'Barter System' to buy and sell items they have created. That means, a farmer used to sell farm products to a cobbler in return of the footwear. But as the society grew, the demand for these things also grew and these individual people found very difficult to cope up with the demand. Here came the concept of 'Factory', a 'Job' and 'Salary'. Factory was a place where many individuals with different expertise started working (or trading their time for money) as a team to produce products in large quantities which satisfied the demand of the people in the society.

In earlier days, schools were not present for everyone and the skills were taught or learnt by kids while working on their family trade. As time moved on, current education system was created, schools were formed to teach various subjects to be able to create 'employees' to support this 'Factory' system.

People started moving from villages to cities in search of jobs. People became comfortable in this 'Job life' and started settling down in cities. They started their families and their children also started going to schools where they get same education to support this 'factory system'. And the race began...

Life path set

As we saw, children started following a charter designed by their parents. At a certain age, it starts going to school, learning different subjects, gives exams, moves from one grade to next. Considering that the world around has become competitive, child is pushed to learn 'Extra Curricular skills' like dancing, singing, drawing, playing a sport etc. Its entire day is kept busy. Continuing this path, child passes through few 'milestone examinations' like 10th Grade and 12th Grade. Post this, it chooses a path to get a University certificate in a stream (graduation or a diploma etc.) to be prepared to contribute to the 'Corporate World'. The goal is to get a good job, earn good salary, enjoy a good lifestyle and be 'successful' in life.

Ideally, we should focus on Strengths rather than spending (wasting) time on improving on weaknesses

The main problem in our education system is that 'it pushes us to work more on the subjects that we are weak in'. The issue with this is, 'the subject that we are weak in' eats up our time, energy and focus that we could have given to further develop the subject that we are good at'. But since the entire system is designed around getting a certificate by learning all the subjects even though students may or may not have any interest in some of them. So, system is designed to 'get us a job' and not 'make us learn'. This is the key reason; we are seeing so many students are not getting jobs even after completing their education. If we dig further into this problem, we will find that, students have 'passed the exams' but haven't really 'understood' the subjects. This is because they didn't have 'interest' in those subjects. Their soul and heart were not there. You got what I am saying. In short, our system is focused on creating certified educated people but have simply ignored to create 'knowledgeable Skilled' people. And that's why, we are seeing heavy shortage of 'skilled' people around.

Success

Success is different for different people. For a few, it can be wealth earned, for some, it can be name, fame and money, it may be accolades, medals, certificates etc. for some and some may feel successful, if they achieve a good health, able to help others and get peace of mind.

Whatever, you name it, success is really the internal satisfaction, peace and sense of fulfillment that one gets by doing one's work. Success can be measured at our work or profession level or it can span across entire life. We see many successful people around. But again, there will be different successful people for different individuals since the measuring stick for success varies. But in any case, if we observe and study these successful people, we can see that, majority of these people have one thing in common and that is *they did what they loved and were good at and became successful*. In other terms, we can say that these people ALWAYS followed their passion and achieved great success. So, we may conclude that, if you do what you love (or love what you do) then chances of becoming successful is High.

* What is Passion? *

All this while, we are hearing the word 'Passion'. But what 'Passion', really is?

In simple terms, Passion is a 'strong love' for a profession, art or skill.

As defined in 'Wikipedia', Passion is a feeling of intense enthusiasm towards or compelling desire for someone or something. Passion can range from eager interest in or admiration for an idea, proposal, or cause; to enthusiastic enjoyment of an interest or activity; to strong attraction, excitement, or emotion towards a person.

Passion is a powerful force in accomplishing anything you set your mind to, and in experiencing work and **life** the fullest extent possible. Ultimately, **passion** is the driving force behind success and happiness that allows us all to live better **lives**.

To understand, passion, better, let us look at life of any person. After completing education, mainly graduation or something similar, one becomes qualified to get a job. Some do get a job after going through multiple stages of selection process. While some who are not good at studies cannot even pass the exams. But they have some hidden talents and skills which they nurture and ultimately become successful than their friends who got the job.

Now, out of the students who get a job, only a few of them become successful in their job. To develop a career or grow in a job requires lot of energy, focus, perseverance and many people don't get enough of these qualities and eventually don't succeed in their career. Here, when I say success, I mean, grow the corporate ladder, getting salary growth etc.

In the above example, we can see 3 types of students. First, who, get a job and become successful in the job life. Second, who do not pass the exams but still work on their talents and achieve success. And third are those, who get a job but fail in the job because they cannot perform to their fullest in that. So, this type of people neither see success in the job nor in any other field of their choice since it's too late for them to try things out.

When we ask question, why this happens to this third type of people? The main reason we can see, they don't Love what they are doing or don't have *passion* about what they are doing.

When one says, I have passion for something, it means that one's mind and soul are in congruence for the work at hand. And when our mind and soul work together, our body too responds in agreement, giving us the required energy, enthusiasm and stamina to perform to our fullest. In fact, if our soul is completely in the work, then universal powers also readily help us in what we do, resulting great Success in that work.

Now, don't think that I am saying that passion helps in a particular area. i.e. in a job or a business etc. People succeed in any field if they are passionate about what they are doing. After all, job, business or anything else we do, are different ways of earning a living or serving the society we live in. That's why, we can also see many family businesses fail, after handing over the business to the next generation. Here, one key reason is the lack of passion for the same business, in the next generation, that earlier generation had built with passion.

Due to lack of our soul and heart in our work (lack of passion), we just work superficially and that reflects in our output. We are physically present at our work area, but our mind is always wandering elsewhere. Our superiors can immediately make this out and that results in lesser salary raise and/or no promotion or even resulting in a job loss.

If, we don't love what we are doing, long hours at work, bother us, we cannot sustain the workload resulting into stress. Our soul passes this stress signal (that you are not loving what you are doing) to our body and our body reacts in the form of work fatigue that in turn results in severe health issues.

Why this happens? Fundamentally, our soul is 'always in search of happiness with our actions' (finding happiness from within). So, when it doesn't find happiness with our work or our actions, it tries to find other sources to be happy. There is a mismatch between, what are we supposed to be doing and what we are actually doing. This results in stress, anxiety, depression and many other anomalies.

So, in short, we ALL should find our 'Passion' OR 'Niche' OR 'Love' or whatever you name it, that makes our soul happy. As, I said earlier, you can find it in the salaried job role that you are doing, the Business that you are running or any other profession that you are doing to earn a living. Different people can have different passions, it's just a matter of finding it and working on it.

We can see tons of people around us, who followed their passion and achieved success. Many great artists, actors, players, businesspersons have mentioned this in their autobiography, interviews that they had passion for their work which helped them to attain the heights of their career. Lata Mangeshkar, Kishore Kumar, Shah Rukh Khan, Steve Jobs, Arnold Schwarzenegger, Sachin Tendulkar, Virat Kohli, Ritesh Agarwal (OYO Founder and CEO), Michael Jordon and many successful people have dedicated their successes to their 'Passion'.

Let us hear from some of the famous personalities about their passion...

Arnold Schwarzenegger

A motivational speech by Arnold Schwarzenegger shows us that we must stay passionate to the things we love, as when we love what we do everything can fall into place.

Have a vision. You have to have direction and focus, or you will drift away from whatever you wish to accomplish. Follow your passion no matter what happens – don't let anything stop you or anyone tell you it's not possible. If this happens it most certainly will become impossible. Make sure that you always do something you love. Find out what it is that drives you forward so you don't lose sight of what really makes you come alive.

Don't listen to the naysayers. Whenever you get that negativity from people, use it as ammunition to spur you on not make you give in. If you can think something, it can be achieved – all its takes is the dedication to see the tasks through. Constantly strive to improve yourself each day and slowly build up new skills to excel at anything you want. Organize your time and use your free moments to really make them count.

Make sure people know about what you are doing. Don't think too much on a Plan B – make sure that there is no doubt in what you are doing and make that happen without a second thought. Don't have a safety net and watch how much better your results will be. If you fail, pick yourself up and push on. It is the only way to win.

Jeff Bezos

CEO and Chairman of Amazon, Jeff Bezos talks about Finding your passion, to have a calling and you'll never workday in your life. Have meaning in your lives. Take things one step at a time and progress each day to see results.

Fall down and get back up, face adversity head on and be proud of the hard work you achieve. Make the choice to work tough to get where you want to go. Minimize the number of regrets you have and find your path to your own satisfaction.

Amazon and Blue Origin founder Jeff Bezos say you don't get to pick your passions.

Passions, "they pick you," Bezos says in a Blue Origin video recently posted on YouTube.

"I think we all have passions, and you don't get to choose them. But you have to be alert to them," explains Bezos. "You have to be looking for them."

Bezos says his passion is space: "Ever since I was 5 years old — that's when Neil Armstrong stepped onto the surface of the moon — I've been passionate about space, rockets, rocket engines, space travel."

Back then, says Bezos, "The idea of going to the moon was so impossible that people actually used it as a metaphor for impossibility. What I would hope you would take away from that is that anything you set your mind to, you can do."

Steve Jobs

In 1997, Steve Jobs returned to Apple after a 12-year absence. The company he had co-founded was running out of cash and close to bankruptcy. Jobs held a staff meeting and explained the role passion would play in revitalizing the brand:

Apple is not about making boxes for people to get their jobs done, although we do that well. Apple is about something more. Its core value is that we believe that people with passion can change the world for the better. The simple phrase -- "people with passion can change the world" -- holds the secret to entrepreneurial success. Nearly a decade later, in 2005, Jobs returned to the theme in his famous commencement speech at Stanford University.

"You've got to find what you love," Jobs said. "The only way to do great work is to love what you do. If you haven't found it yet, keep looking. Don't settle. As with all matters of the heart, you'll know when you find it."

Passion is everything. Following your passion is the secret to overcoming the setbacks all entrepreneurs face and it builds resistance against the inevitable naysayers who will question your vision. It's also an essential ingredient in successful communication. If you're not passionate about your ideas, nobody else will be. Successful entrepreneurs are abundantly passionate -- but not necessarily about the product. They're passionate about their missions. They're passionate about what their products or services mean to the lives of their customers. They're passionate about changing the world or disrupting an established category. For example, Jobs wasn't passionate about computer hardware. He was passionate about building tools that would help people unleash their personal creativity.

Howard Schultz (Former CEO, Starbucks)

In an interview, Starbucks CEO Howard Schultz, we spoke for more than an hour and he didn't bring up the word "coffee."

"Coffee is the product, but it's not the business we're in," he told. He says "We are not in a business of filling bellies, we are in a business of filling souls'

Schultz built an empire from scratch precisely because he wasn't as passionate about the product as he was about "creating a third place between work and home." Anyone can sell a cup of coffee. It takes a true innovator to create an experience.

Elon Musk (CEO of Tesla Motors and SpaceX)

It's expected that you need to go "all-in" when launching a business — long hours, stress, overcoming obstacles and uphill battles — but there comes a point when no amount of caffeine and luck can help you push through. No matter how earth-shattering your idea is and how flawlessly you execute, there will undoubtedly be several occasions where things will just simply go wrong. And not just kind of wrong– I'm talking horribly, gut-wrenchingly wrong, where your fight-or-flight instincts will try to convince you you're about to actually die.

And when you hit this point — the metaphorical brick wall — which everyone hits eventually, there's a decision to make, shut down or move forward. There is always a path forward, it just depends how creative you want to get, and how creative you get is usually a function of how bad you want it. But even when there is a path forward, the tasks can seem so daunting that no amount of money, no disappointed investor or no upset customer can fuel your efforts– at this point, passion is the only thing that can help you push through.

Mark Zuckerberg (Facebook founder and CEO)

Zuckerberg has always been fascinated by building systems that connect people... Yes, Zuckerberg has always been passionate about using technology to connect people, but he has also put in the hard work to achieve it. Because of this passion, he could resist multiple buyout offers from the giants like Microsoft, Yahoo and other investors. He was so passionate about his work that he continued running the company and grew it to the world's largest social media company. In fact, he created a whole industry as 'Social Media'. If he would not have been passionate and focused, he could have easily sold it, earned billions and could have led peaceful life.

Sachin Tendulkar (Bharat Ratna, a Cricket Legend)

It all starts with #LoveWhatYoDoSachin's passion for the game is well known to his legions of fans. In the past, the Master Blaster has compared playing cricket to visiting a temple. Sachin's passion for the cricket is also borne out by former India cricketer and fellow Mumbaikar Chandrakant Pandit who observed him from an early age. "All he wanted to do was to play cricket. Till his last day in cricket, he retained the passion, and the hunger of that little boy who was impatient for his turn at the nets," Pandit said in an interview following Sachin's retirement in 2013. Career lesson: If you want to excel in your career, you've first got to be passionate about the job you do. Having your passion as a career intensifies focus, fosters creativity and innovation, and inspires you to pursue excellence just like the Master Blaster. On the other hand, doing a job just for the sake of it could negatively impact performance, impede career growth, and take a toll on your physical and mental well-being.

Shah Rukh Khan (famous Indian Bollywood actor)

Shah Rukh Khan, a prime example of a self-made star in the Hindi film industry, shared his take on the importance of money, making it big in life and following your passion.

According to Shah Rukh, everyone needs to have some passion, otherwise life can become very tedious. He added that if your passion can become your work, that's good. According to him, age doesn't play a role in pursuing one's passion. To illustrate this, he cited the example of Boman Irani who started working as an actor in movies in his 40s. "You have one life, so take one shot and do the things you want to do. And even if you fail at least you know you tried."

Just to summarize, Passion helps us in following ways…

- ✓ Helps our soul to find happiness that it is looking for
- ✓ Gives focus in our actions
- ✓ Helps our body and mind to perform well even in tough situations (long hours, negative feedback from others, temporary failures etc.)
- ✓ Gives you excitement to work, day over day
- ✓ Motivates people around you to work with you
- ✓ Forces, universal energies to help us achieve success

22 | Your Life Your Way

#MissionPassion™

Now that, we have understood the importance of passion to achieve success, let us see how to find our passion and how to make it a 'Mission' of your life by converting the same into a career. I have termed this entire process as '#MissionPassion'

'MissionPassion' is a program or a process designed by the author of this book, to help people to identify, nurture and develop their passion into a career to live a life to its fullest. It's a 3-step process...

Identify Passion ➡ **Define Mission Passion Statement** ➡ **Convert Psasion into Career**

Step 1 – to identify one's passion

Step 2 – to create a '**MissionPassion Statement**' for oneself

Step 3 – to convert your passion into a successful career

Step 1 – to identify one's passion

How to identify and develop your Passion

As we saw earlier, passion is a 'strong love' for something. So, it is something that comes from within, which means, it is already present inside us. It's just a matter of finding it. You may have observed that, few traits or skills come naturally to us i.e. we are good at art or skill from our childhood even though we have not received any formal training for it. So, if we cultivate this skill further, we can become expert at it and turn it into a career.

As a parent, you can follow these 5 steps to identify and develop 'Passion' in your kid.

- Observe which skill comes naturally to your child. What is it's born talent? Which subject child takes interest in?
- Develop that interest by creating environment or providing avenues
- Continue support to be expert in it
- Help develop it into a Career
- Keep sharpening the skill

Adults can identify their True Passion by asking these questions...

- o   What, you as an individual want to achieve (purpose) or want to be known for, before you die?
- o   What is your Bigger Life cause?
- o   Why are you here on this earth?
- o   What motivates you to get up from your bed every day?
- o   Which work gives you true happiness?
- o   What is the single most thing that you love even if you don't get returns for the same, even if you face adversities in the path, even if you must work longer or even if you have to walk alone on the path?

After answering these questions, you will be able to find that one skill, the niche, your true passion.

Step 2 - to define your 'Mission Passion Statement'

This is the most important step in your journey. This step must be done with all the focus since this is going to be your guiding post throughout your future.

"Okay, are you ready? Let's start."

You may have seen that, organization publish it's 'Mission Statement'. Mission Statement is a short statement of why the organization exists. It helps them to stick to the 'Larger Cause' of their existence. So, in this step, you are going to write your 'MissonPassion' statement, to help you stick to your passion journey, your purpose of life.

A typical organization Mission Statement has 3 parts. What a company does? Why it does it? How it does it?

For e.g. Here is a sample mission statement...

Our company provides High quality (How) educational services (What?) that allow children to experience success in learning and success in life. (Why)

In the similar lines, I want you to define, your 'MissionPassion Statement'.

How to do it? Let's see how you can use the above example to define your own 'MissionPassion Statement'

Let us assume that you are passionate about music, singing or playing any musical instrument.

Considering this is your passion, you can define your 'MissionPassion' statement like below.

- ❖ *I/We, give Magical musical experience (what) by reviving old melodies (how) that will help music lovers to forget their worries (Why)*

Let's take another example.

Say, you are passionate about 'Cricket Coaching', then you can define your passion statement like...

- ❖ *I create (how) and nurture best cricketing talent (what) to play for our Country (why)*

Exercise for you- Take a piece of paper and try to write your 'MissionPassion' statement on it

This way you can write your own 'MissonPassion' statement. This statement will act as a guidepost throughout your career journey. So, spend good amount of time writing this statement. Remember, this is going to be with you for entire life so do it carefully. You may have to do multiple iterations before finalizing it, but It's okay. Now, once you finalize the statement, type it in big font, print it on A4 or A3 paper and put/paste it somewhere, where ONLY YOU can see it. See and read it daily before starting your workday and before you go to bed at night. Internalize it so that it sinks into your subconscious mind. While you read it, read it with emotions. This will help to strengthen your commitment.

Now that you have defined your 'MissionPassion Statement', let us proceed to see how you can turn your passion into a career.

Step 3 – to convert passion into a successful career

Congratulations on completing step 2. Now it's time to act on the next step, i.e. converting your passion into a career. A Career is something that helps us to earn our living, giving us identity in the society. It can be a job, a self-employment, a business etc.

Let us see how each one of these can be built based on your passion.

Convert your passion into Career

Many people feel stuck in a situation, where, they are doing a job, but are not happy with the same. This happens typically to the people in their late 30s or 40s, when they have a job and are earning well but cannot leave that job because they need to feed their family. What to do in this case?

- Start part time (after office, spare time, holidays, weekends etc.) learning and practicing your passion

I truly believe that your future is heavily dependent on 'how you use your spare time'. That means, if you use your spare time wisely, chances of you getting success are pretty high. This is because, we all have same time available per day so, it all depends on how we make the best use of it. That makes all the difference in the world. So, start part time with your passion and taste the waters before you dive deep.

- Start building network of likeminded people

I also believe that your success or failure depends on the friends or company you keep. So now, that you started part time working on your passion, you can start meeting people who are already doing this full time and has done well in this area. Join groups on social media and outside, start posting your thoughts to get you some recognition. Network with them, be with them and you will get great insights in the area that you are soon going to enter

- Get some degree or certification or something that recognizes your skill

We live in a world where people value a certificate or something that approves your skills. So, try to get a certification to authenticate your knowledge and skills.

- Try and get a job to practice your passion and grow further

Once you have all the earlier steps completed, try to find a job that will give you an opportunity to implement your skills. Now, remember, in the initial period, you may not get a salary matching your current job but certainly you will get an opportunity to practice your passion. And soon your interest and energy will get you desired results.

Passion into a career when you are just starting off

This life condition happens to students who are just starting their career. For them, starting to work on their passion is bit difficult because they need to first convince their parents for the same. But in fact, this is the best opportunity for them to prepare themselves to sell their passion. If they can sell to their family, chances are good that they can sell to the outside world. So, first do some homework and find out how you can achieve success and happiness continuing your passion. Once you cross the hurdle, start working on it before even you graduate or complete your formal education.

Following below steps would help to build your passion career.

1. Learn in depth, the art, skill that you are passionate about

    It's always better to be, master of one instead of being 'jack of all trade'. So, learn and gain more expertise in the skill, trade that you are passionate about.

2. Get some recognized degree or something similar from a University.

This is a world where there is a value of a certificate or something that approves your skills. So, try and get a certification to authenticate your knowledge and skills.

3. Practice your skills

    You must have heard the saying, 'practice makes a person perfect'. This is applicable here too. So, practice your skills until you are satisfied with your own skills. Try to find opportunities to practice whenever and wherever you can.

4. Get recognition from people and develop your personal brand

    Try to get recognized within the circles of people who are in the same trade that you are. Perform to such an extent that they will recognize your name with the skill.

5. Get a job of your passion

    Once you have all the above steps completed, try to find a job that will give you a platform to demonstrate your skills. Now, remember, in the initial period, you may not get big salary but certainly you will get an opportunity to practice your passion. Keep on practicing and your interest and energy will get you desired results in short span of time.

A Word of caution: During this period, you may see or get or be asked to get a job in other skills/areas of your formal education that can give you higher earning potential, but you still need to stick to the one that you have passion for.

Now, let us see, how you can start 'on your own' with your passion.

Passion into a 'Self Employment' career

Self-Employment is something where You work alone (an Independent Contributor) to help others with your knowledge or skills. For e.g. Consultants, Coach, Teacher, Electrician, Plumber, Mechanic etc. fall in this category. Typically, this is for the people who have a skill and they trade their skill and time to earn a living.

This can be a good choice for the people who are currently employees and have a good knowledge and experience in certain field and want to start on their own. Follow these steps to get into a 'Self Employment' career.

Identify the clients/customers who need your skills and are ready to pay for your skills

This is important step because there should be someone out there who needs your skills and is ready to pay for the same. Hint- you might have already worked with some of those customers while working in your job. You can start with few of them to begin with.

Start with small assignments in your spare time to practice your skills

You can start doing small tasks here and there for Free, in your spare time to practice and demonstrate your expertise. This will give you opportunity to try and fail a few times. This in turn will build your confidence to handle bigger assignments in future.

Start building your network of customers, vendors etc.

As you keep doing the small odd assignments, start building your customer base. Ensure that you are keeping in touch with your customers to get you similar jobs in the future. Also, start building a network of partners who have complementary skills and are ready to work with you and recommend your name to their clients. Also create contacts with the vendors who can give you good raw material, services that you procure with them and that too on credit if required.

1. Get recommendations or referrals from your customers

    Do not forget or hesitate to ask for some referrals from your existing customers. Their experience working with you can fetch you more customers.

2. Develop your personal brand

    Keep practicing your skills and aim to attain such a level that you will get a brand identity linked to your expertise and work quality.

Passion into starting a Business

Now, this is perhaps the most challenging shift for those who are currently doing a job. It is because, when you are in a job or self-employed, you are performing your role and are responsible only for your area of expertise.

But, in a business, you are responsible for entire business. You must wear multiple Hats (perform multiple roles) in the initial period of the business. But don't lose heart, if you are passionate about your work, you will learn along the way and/or will get good people to work on the areas of the business that you are not good at. In the business world the most important skills one should have is the 'Leadership skills' and 'working with people'. And, if you don't like working with people and if you feel that you can do the best job than anyone else then, I would not recommend you start a business. You can opt for a 'Self Employment career' instead.

But you still have decided to start a business, my suggestion is to find a good mentor to guide you on your way to Entrepreneurship. Mentor will help you, right from starting your business, business planning, building strategies, getting investors, finding and building a right team and partners etc. And all this while you can focus on your core skill so that your personal brand helps to boost your business brand.

Now, we will see the steps that you need to follow in order to start a business

1. Identify what problem in the society you can solve with your skills and find customers who are ready to pay for your skills

   Entrepreneur is the one who solves a problem that is there in the society or fulfills the need of the society. So, as first step, you need to look for the problems and the needs that you can work on. Then look for the customers who are ready to pay for the products or services that you are going to offer. You can get this information through online search, by doing surveys and by starting with some proof of concept of your offering to check how the market receives the same. This is called as MVP (Minimum Viable Product). This means you can develop the offering with basic features to test the market before you go with full-fledged services.

2. Start small to begin with

   You can start selling your products in your local market. This will improve your selling skills which is the most important skill for an Entrepreneur. This will give you opportunity to try and fail a few times. This in turn will build your confidence to handle bigger customers base in future

3. Start building your network of customers, vendors etc.

   As you keep selling in the local market, start building your customer base. Ensure that you are keeping in touch with your customers to get repeat sales in the future. Also, start building a network of partners who have complementary products/services and are ready to work with you and recommend your business to their customers. Also create contacts with the vendors who can give you good raw material, services that you procure with them and that too on credit if required.

4. Find investors who will be ready to invest in your company

   Now that you are developing a business, you must build a team to perform various tasks and develop systems and processes and all these require capital. You must start with your own funds and the funds from your family and friends to begin with. But once you have customers and your business start showing results you can start looking for investors.

5. Build a business and a team to expand your customer base.

   Business is a system (team, processes etc.) that works following defined process to serve customers and gain profit for the investors. So, when you get the investments, you must start building systems to not only serve the customers but also to get new customers.

6. Get recommendations or referrals from your customers

   In the business, developing a 'Loyalty program' is very important because it is always good to get business from your existing customer than finding a new one. It is believed that Businesses spend 7 times more cash to win new customer than to retain customers. So, carefully design programs that will help to win customers loyalty for your brand.

7. Develop your Business brand

   Brand is not only a logo or a name but it's a promise that a brand gives and keeps to its customers. So, ensure that each of your department or areas within your business, is keeping your promise to your customers.

8. Keep building systems and processes to streamline the operations

As we saw earlier, business is not about you, but, it's about systems and processes. So, always focus on setting up processes and streamlining the operations. Always keep in mind that, McDonalds is not known for serving the best tasting burger, but it is certainly known as the best system to serve that burger consistently across the world every day.

9. Keep your marketing and advertising ACTIVE to get more customers

    This is very important area but the most ignored one. Especially, when the businesses are not performing well and the sales is lower, the first department to get a cost cut is Marketing. But this is not a good choice. In fact, you can try to streamline your operations to save your operating cost but never reduce the marketing spend. You may make it more focused for your market segment. After all, people must see you, hear you, feel your brand before they buy from you.

10. Keep an eye on cashflow

    Now this is 'the most important' point. Cashflow is the blood flow of the business. I have seen good businesses fail, just because they couldn't manage the cashflow. So, please make sure that even if you have good sales and good customers, don't lose focus on cash inflow and investments coming in. How can one run without fuel in his tummy?

After, hearing all this, you may feel overwhelmed and might have already started self-doubting and may ask me...

"Will I be able to do all this?

OR

"Will I be able to earn enough, if I don't take up a job and start with my business instead?"

OR

"What if, I take up a job in the field that I love but has less pay as compared to the one I can get with my current degree?"

OR

"What if, I start part time but cannot balance between job and business?

To all these questions, a simple answer is, 'YES', you can do it. See this way. You are anyway going to do or already doing something even though you don't love it, right? So, why, on earth you think, you won't be able to do something or succeed into something that you love? On the contrary, chances of your success in the work that you are passionate about are far greater than the one you are doing that you don't love.

So, keep faith, create a plan, find a good mentor and take it one day at a time. If you do this, you will achieve the success that you were always looking for. And this success will be for YOU to cherish and not for showing to others. The great feeling of fulfillment will be incomparable to any other happiness.

Remember, there is a need of everything in this world, it's just that we need to find it and then solve it. Would people in India have thought that one day, water will be sold in bottles and people would buy it? Had anyone thought that people would buy a phone not just to call but do many other activities? And had they thought that one would pay Rs. 50,000/- for a phone?

So, don't worry keep the lights on and you will find your way.

Be-Do-Have Principle

Many of us create a 'To Do' list and follow it regularly. We work (Do) to achieve something (Have). Let's say, if someone wants to reduce weight (Have), that person follows diet plans (Do). But does everyone get the desired results? Not always. Few could not follow the diet consistently and gain weight again. This happens because people follow 'Do-Have' part but don't work on the 'Be' part and fail to achieve the desired output. This means, if you want to 'Have' something you not only have to 'Do' but also 'Be' that person. You must change your mindset and internalize the thought of the 'Have' and act on it to achieve the desired results.

Focus

Keep a complete focus on your 'PASSION'. Don't get distracted by the challenges in the initial phase of the shift. Keep faith in your choice and abilities and work consciously one day at a time to grow your skills and customers. Keep visiting your '#MissionPassion Statement' daily morning to remind you of what you are set to achieve.

Also, try to set up short term, mid-term and long-term goals with the help of your mentor.

Join some networking groups on social sites as well as outside related to your passion, to get known in the circles and to improve your skills.

Try to start with small assignments to begin with which will help you gain the confidence to go for bigger ones later.

Keep yourself motivated with some powerful quotes on 'Following your Passion' by successful people…

1. "You can do anything as long as you have the passion, the drive, the focus, and the support." — Sabrina Bryan

2. "I have to face life with a newly found passion. I must rediscover the irresistible will to learn, to live and to love." — Andrea Bocelli

3. "If you don't love what you do, you won't do it with much conviction or passion." — Mia Hamm

4. "Follow your own passion—not your parents', not your teachers'—yours." — Robert Ballard

5. "If you feel like there's something out there that you're supposed to be doing, if you have a passion for it, then stop wishing and just do it." —Wanda Sykes

6. "There is no passion to be found playing small—in settling for a life that is less than the one you are capable of living." — Nelson Mandela

7. "Passion is energy. Feel the power that comes from focusing on what excites you." — Oprah Winfrey

8. "Nothing is as important as passion. No matter what you want to do with your life, be passionate." — Jon Bon Jovi

9. "A great leader's courage to fulfill his vision comes from passion, not position." — John C. Maxwell

10. "I would rather die of passion than of boredom." — Vincent Van Gogh

11. "If you can't figure out your purpose, figure out your passion. For your passion will lead you right into your purpose." — Bishop T.D. Jakes

12. "Chase your passion, not your pension." — Denis Waitley

13. "Without passion man is a mere latent force and possibility, like the flint which awaits the shock of the iron before it can give forth its spark." — Henri Frederic Amiel

14. "Only passions, great passions, can elevate the soul to great things." — Denis Diderot

15. "You have to be burning with an idea, or a problem, or a wrong that you want to right. If you're not passionate enough from the start, you'll never stick it out." — Steve Jobs

16. "Chase down your passion like it's the last bus of the night." —Terri Guillemets

17. "One person with passion is better than forty people merely interested." — E. M. Forster

18. "You can't fake passion." — Barbara Corcoran

19. "I have no special talents. I am only passionately curious." — Albert Einstein

> **Note**: We conduct separate mentoring programs for 'Young Entrepreneurs' who wish to start their own ventures'.
>
> ...To know more, please contact on +91 8879975958 or email to yourbigleap@gmail.com

> **Note**: We also conduct separate programs for 'Young graduates', for how to create a personal brand and grow quickly in the job ladder.
>
> ...To know more, please contact on +91 8879975958 or email to yourbigleap@gmail.com

* Passion to Success Story of Raj *

This is a story based on true events occurred in the life of an average person, Raj (name changed) and his success journey of 'MissionPassion'.

Raj was born in 1970's, in a middle-class family in a small suburb of Mumbai in Maharashtra State in India. He was living with his parents and elder brother in a small one room kitchen setup. Though his parents were not rich, they were earning enough to get Raj and his brother, a good education. Raj was good in his studies. Though, not a top ranker, he used to get good marks throughout his school days. Both of his parents were Government employees. When Raj was in 6th grade, his mother opted for a Voluntary Retirement Scheme (VRS) so that she can stay at home and look after her children and their studies. Since, she was not doing a job (although getting some pension), she started doing some part time work as Post office agent to earn commission and helping the family financially. She used to help people get the savings policy, submit their forms and money into the post office, collect and deliver the certificates to the client and get commission. She used to do this in the afternoon after finishing all the house chores. This created an impact on Raj's thinking about women can work part time to earn and support the family and still can give enough time to kids. His father also, in his spare time, used to do some odd jobs like selling washing machines, selling air conditioner attachments that help to keep air rotating. (in those days of 1980's, room air conditioners didn't have the flaps that rotate to keep air circulating. So, this attachment used to be fitted to keep air circulating). On weekends and holidays, he used to go to different offices, give the product demo and try to get orders. Maniar times, people refuse to buy, and his visit was wasted. But he kept trying. His father too tried his hands at taking 'catering contracts' and successfully handled that business as well. But all these, were done as part time, keeping his permanent job on. Raj was observing all this and his thoughts of doing some business were getting concrete. It was engraved on his mind that one needs to have multiple sources of income. This was the time when many private companies were closing because of the 'workers' strike' and his father didn't want to leave his permanent Government job to focus on any of these part time businesses.

Not able to continue on Passion (OR Interests)

Raj used to play 'gulley Cricket' like any other boy in that era. But certainly, he was better than many of his friends and kids of his age. He liked to follow his idol, Sunil Gavaskar. His cousin brother who was a Cricket coach himself saw Raj's game and advised his father to send him to some good coach. But this was not possible because his father thought that Raj may get distracted from his studies if he starts playing cricket. So, the passion for cricket never went beyond local gully cricket. (please note that at this vary time somewhere in Mumbai, a star cricketer named Sachin Tendulkar, was being trained to become The Cricket Legend).

Raj was also a good singer and used to sing Kishore Kumar (sung for super star Mr. Amitabh Bachchan) songs well. But he was shy so was not able to exhibit his skills in front of others. His father used to push Raj to sing but he used to run away. So, even this talent or skill was not developed further.

In due course, Raj passed his tenth grade with decent marks and opted for 'Science' stream. His father was from technical background and of the opinion that technical skills will help Raj to earn bread and butter better than other streams like commerce or arts. Raj started his college but couldn't get enough marks in

PCM (Physics, Chemistry and Mathematics) in 12th grade Board Exams to get an admission to Engineering in a good college in Mumbai. But it was already decided that Raj will do Mechanical or Electrical Engineering since these were core branches of Engineering stream and if Raj does any of these, he can get a job easily.

Admission to Engineering

So, by paying high fees Raj got an admission in a private engineering college in Pune for Mechanical Engineering stream. For the first time, he had to stay away from him home, family and friends for 4 years. But he was ready for this challenge since he wanted to fulfill his father's dream of his son getting a degree in Engineering. Although good in studies, Raj struggled to focus and finish his engineering since he didn't find the subjects interesting and failed in few subjects in few semesters. Eventually, he completed his engineering and got a degree in 5 years instead of 4 years.

But any way, Raj had fulfilled his father's dream. But one thing that went well for Raj by staying away from the family is that he became an independent person. He was able to take decisions independently and learned to take responsibility of his decisions. He also learnt to live and face adverse conditions. This helped him in future a lot.

Now, the next bigger challenge was to get a job. Since, he didn't pass with good grades, Raj didn't get a job through campus placement. And since, he wanted to come back home, he didn't try to get a job in Pune. Raj was struggling to get a job in Mumbai. He used to look for job advertisements in newspapers, placement agencies and apply but no luck. By this time, his elder brother, was already doing a job. One of his friends helped Raj to get a job as apprentice trainee in a chemical company in

Mumbai. Raj started and got a good experience working on the chemical plant projects with good mentors. But this was for one year only and again the same question of getting a permanent job, struck.

Back to Pune

One day, Raj's Engineering college mate, called him to inform that he is working with a good engineering company in Pune and there is a job opening which matches Raj's experience and he has scheduled an interview. Raj was overjoyed. He appeared for the interview and got selected. He came back and was waiting for the offer letter and was eager to join. But...his struggle period was not over yet. The company Chief decided to put a hold on his offer and asked HR to see if there is any suitable candidate inside the company first who can fill up that position. Raj was shattered. His Diwali was not as happy as it should have been. His other friends were getting good job opportunities, but he was struggling, He was angry with everyone now and with himself. He was frustrated and was cursing his luck. Weeks passed by, and one afternoon, his Pune friend called again.

"Raj, I have good news for you. Your appointment letter is with me right now. I will courier it to you and you need to sign a copy and send it back to the HR.", he said.

Raj couldn't believe his own ears. He was happy for the same. He was ready to take up this job thinking that now things will be smooth for him, which obviously were not.

Raj moved back to Pune. He started with this new job. He got to learn many new things here and met many good people. But in couple of years, he started feeling that work is monotonous and his experience is limited to a small area of the industry. Also, he observed that his boss unnecessarily making him sit late hours without any urgent work. This bothered Raj a lot. He was no more enjoying the work but just working to get some salary at the end of every month. He tried to get a new job in the same field, but he was getting reply as his experience is into small part of the industry and is insufficient to get entry into a big company.

Desire to switch to IT career

Those were Y2K days (year 2000) and many IT companies were getting 'Y2K' projects from its clients across the globe. There were many Indian IT companies who were providing training to the Engineering graduates from any stream and giving them IT jobs. One day, Raj met one such college friend who was not doing well in his Mechanical field job. Raj was surprised to hear that his friend got a training and job in an IT company. Raj was again upset with himself and his luck. To make things worse for him, he got to know one day that this friend was in Paris on 31st December eve. He had travelled to Paris for a project for 3 months. "Now, this is too much...", he said in frustration to his colleague, "what we are doing here and see where others are going? We need to do some course in IT and switch to IT".

We too can go abroad for project work someday," he said. His friend nodded in agreement.

They joined a training course to learn programming and completed the 2 months course. Now, coding had become his passion and he was doing programming all the time, whenever and wherever he can. He did some programming assignments at his workplace as well, but still, was not able to get a real opportunity to enter IT.

Non-IT to IT

Raj kept his search on. One day he saw an advertisement from a company which was offering a 2 months training followed by a job for Non-IT people. But for the same, he had to leave his current job, spend a good amount of money for the course and to buy a computer for practicing at home. This was a crucial decision to make but he was now ready to take up any risk for this opportunity. He said to himself," This is a good opportunity and if I don' take the risk now, then I may have to wait for long and by the time, it will be too late". His parent also supported him, and he returned back from Pune leaving his permanent job.

Raj started learning tools and programming languages and after two and half months of learning and practicing, he was able to do coding and design websites. As agreed by the company, they provided him a job to implement what he has learnt. But the salary was very less as compared to his earlier one. But now, he has decided to dedicate his full energy and someday fly abroad and work there.

Network Marketing

Raj was always interested in doing business. While he was learning computer coding, he listened to an audio track of 'Mr.

Robert Kiyosaki' where he was talking about his book 'Rich Dad Poor Dad' and also talking about how one can learn about money, sales and business world by working in some good 'Network Marketing company'. Raj was highly impressed by thoughts of Mr. Kiyosaki and read all his books one by one. In the meanwhile, he heard about an opportunity to work with a Network Marketing Company promoting IT related products. Raj joined this company and started his part time career. He kept working at his job but kept learning about business, sales, marketing, investing, communications, team building etc. while working on his network business. He became a good leader and effective salesperson in due course. Although he didn't earn a lot of money but certainly the learning was highly rewarding. Things were going well for some time but later he started observing that the company is not following true network marketing principles and diverting into an investment scheme. He didn't want him and his team to go that direction, so he stopped working for this company.

Risk paid well

Raj's journey into IT was not smooth either. He moved from one company to another but couldn't get the breakthrough opportunity he was looking for. He got a short-term onsite assignment to work in the Middle East in between but the real big opportunity came in when he joined one of the well-known Indian IT companies. They selected him to go to USA and work there. This was what Raj was looking for. His struggle of 5 years has paid off and dream that he saw before leaving his Non-IT job was about to turn into a reality. He could hear those voices which were questioning his decision to leave the job, his decision to start afresh with nothing in hand. For Raj, this was a great sense of achievement. Raj flew to USA, worked there for couple of years and came back. He learnt a lot from that experience.

He got opportunity to read a lot about Entrepreneurship, about great Businesspeople which helped him in future. After coming back, Raj changed his job and joined another big IT company. He climbed the corporate ladder and reached to middle Management level.

Entering Entrepreneurship World

Raj, from the beginning had an Entrepreneurial mindset which he had inherited from his parents. He read a lot about Entrepreneurship, Business, franchising etc. and was looking for something to start implementing his knowledge. He was fascinated by McDonalds and how the fast food chain had developed franchisee system across the world. In those days, he switched his job, but the work was not interesting, and his mind started leaning towards starting a business. So, he started his part time venture, a QSR (Quick Service Restaurant) with a partner who agreed to look after day to day operations and Raj to take care of finance and Business Development. But in the first year itself, he realized that his partner is not so passionate about the business and not as eager to grow business as he was. One reason was because the partner didn't have any financial stake in the business. By now, Raj had burnt lot of cash by taking loans but no luck with the sales. Raj was in dilemma, whether to continue or quit and focus on the job. He continued with the business and his job. But at the same time, he was trying to find a new job where the work is matching his expertise. But even on that front, he didn't get success. He was rejected by dozens of companies. In fact, he was robbed for lacs of rupees by fraudulent placement firms by false promising to provide job in big IT firms. Overall, Raj was at the losing end from all sides. His life was in a complete financial mess. During this time, he found one person who he thought can take care of his QSR operations. This new partner started off well, so Raj took some additional loan from his close friends who readily gave him the money. But bad days were not over yet. One late evening, Raj got a call that this new partner had met with an accident and had to be operated. After the operation, he could not work for another 2-3 months. This was a big blow for Raj, and he lost his remaining hopes completely to continue with this outlet. Finally, he decided to sell his venture. Few people responded but nothing worked out. One day, one person approached Raj and he was interested to take over. But when that person saw the operations for couple of days, he mentioned that he would like to create a new brand altogether and he is ready to work with Raj and his team. Raj was already decided to sell off any way, so he agreed to this proposal. He was so eager to succeed in the business world; that he didn't want to quit but to try new options.

Starting a new- New QSR outlet

As agreed, Raj and his new partners put up some investment and started a new venture, a new brand, a new outlet to serve homely food. Concept was unique and they got good response to start with. But within few months they realized that they are out of cash. This time, his partner got some loan from her relative and the show continued. In the meanwhile, they got a good opportunity to serve 'the Marathi TV celebrities' at their shooting location. This gave them a good brand recognition. Few months went well and again after few months they started facing the same cash crunch.

Things got worse

Raj started facing financial problems as he was paying heavy EMI for his home loan and on the loan taken for business. Things on the business front were not helping solve this problem.

At the other end, he was not enjoying his job as well but had to continue doing it to get that fixed salary every month to pay the EMIs and other expenses. At times, situations were so bad that he had to borrow some money from his partner and friends to keep sufficient balance in the account for the EMI. Even on few months' end, he had to swipe his credit card to make some purchases since there was almost no cash in bank account. He was down, and the pressure was unbearable. He had all possible kinds of debt, a home loan, top up loan, personal loan, Credit Card debt and loan taken from friends. He didn't see any way to repay these loans. The only source of income was his salary which was drying up within first week of the month or so and he had to survive for the remaining month on little money left in the account. Things were going southwards. Still somehow, he survived and continued running his business.

Business was again on the verge of bankruptcy and partners didn't know what to do now. In the meantime, orders were coming but no cash in hand to run the operations. Raj approached one of his colleagues from earlier company to invest some amount and become a partner. She and her husband agreed. But majority of the amount they put in was used to pay annual rent of the space and little cash was left to use for the operations.

Opening First Franchisee

From the day of starting his first venture, Raj was obsessed with Franchising concept. He was very fond of McDonalds and Subway brands and had read and learnt the franchising thoroughly. He now wanted to implement those in real life. So, he started pitching for 'Franchising his homely food outlet' concept. He received few enquiries, but nothing went further than the initial discussions. In the meanwhile, Raj asked his partners to create SOPs for the operations and documenting the recipes etc. There was an enquiry from a friend of his partner. They were shifting to Nashik and wanted to start something. After few rounds of discussions, they finalized to take the franchisee and in the month of January, they signed the contract and handed over a cheque of franchisee fee to the team. This was the dream come true moment for Raj. What he envisioned and strived for, had become a reality.

A New Beginning – Starting a Business Consultancy

All this while, Raj was doing self-assessment about his experiences in the Entrepreneurial world, in network marketing, the mistakes he made, losses he incurred, lessons he learnt and most importantly the knowledge and experience he gained. A thought struck his mind.

He thought to himself, *"There will be many people who want to become Entrepreneurs but may not be aware of, how to start? So, why not to use my knowledge of Business setup and development to help them who are in the same boat I was few years back."*

Raj really got charged up with this idea and decided to start his own 'Business Consultancy'. But he didn't want to just guide people but wanted to 'mentor' them and work with them through their Entrepreneurship journey. He started conceptualizing the overall business plan and various consulting and coaching programs to help different categories of Entrepreneurs and Businesspeople. He thought, *"I made lots of mistakes in starting up and running a business and lost lots of money and time in due course. I need to help budding Entrepreneurs to save their money and time by sharing my knowledge and experience? Will they be interested taking up my services?"* He got his answer and he started promoting his idea on social media to get clients.

Getting First consulting Client

One day, he got a call from a businesswoman who saw his ad on social media and wanted to understand more about his services. She described the problems she is facing, and Raj explained how he can help her. They decided to meet at her office. Raj met her and she was happy to know that Raj can help her expand her business. She was convinced that Raj is the person who can help her not just for the money, but he really wants to help people like her. She asked Raj to send a proposal for his consulting services. Raj was super happy. He was very excited because he had got his first client who was ready to pay for his services. He sent his phase wise services proposal and the businesswoman approved it and paid first phase fees amount. This was again a moment of achievement since what he envisaged was coming true.

Eureka moment - Finding True Passion

At this moment, Raj felt that 'this is it'. He got a strong feeling from within that he has found his true Passion. All this while, he was thinking that his passion was to 'Build and expand Businesses' but now he realized that he was not here for running a business or for the execution, but instead was driven by helping entrepreneurs with innovative business models, coaching, consulting, meeting people, sharing his knowledge. These things were motivating him. This was the 'Eureka' moment for Raj.

It was like his rebirth. He was overjoyed to find out his true purpose, the reason of his presence on the earth. He was there to help others to build businesses and successful careers, educate others about how to lead a happy life, educating young people about how money works and how not only to just earn money but to create wealth.

Raj kept on getting clients. He helped them solve their problems and got few more through their references. Raj cleared off his debt, left his job and continued to help others, earned respect and created wealth. He became richer beyond his wildest dreams and beyond any job that could have helped him to earn that much. He wrote books on Entrepreneurship, Money and Passion. He travelled across the world, kept sharing his knowledge, helping others to achieve their dreams thus living his Passion.

Now, he is mentoring not only businesspeople but also coaching young people to find their passion and educating them about the 'Concept of Money and Entrepreneurship'. He also guides those who are doing job and want to excel in it...

...Raj lived his passion thereafter... when you are starting...?

Some Final Thoughts

I hope this story has motivated you to take that first step. Did you observe in the story, how Raj kept going despite of all the adversities? How he took risks at various phases of his life, like when he moved from Non-IT to IT field, when he started his first business, when he started his second business even after making losses in the first, when he started his consultancy services business even though he had a good paying job. It shows that, if you want to live your passion, there will be difficult times to face, risks to take, hard work to do and long hours to put. But, trust me, the results will be bigger and fulfilling than all these challenges. In fact, your passion will provide you that energy, that stamina, that strong will, that focus and that courage to tackle all the challenges.

A word of caution

#MissionPassion is designed based on my real-life experiences, real life stories like Raj's story and universal principles. But in the market, there are many 'Business Coaches' available, who are offering such programs and charging high fees. Just be cautious to check that 'They are not just Trainers or Advisors, but they are Entrepreneurs and have lived through, what they are preaching.

Here are some suggestions or words of wisdom I would like to share...

Some Final Thoughts | 57

- ✓ Use your spare time to read a lot of books or watch videos about Business, Economics, Entrepreneurship
- ✓ Grow network of like-minded people in your skill niche. Meet those who have already achieved what you are trying to achieve or are doing what you want to do
- ✓ Keep focused on your goal and mission and remind yourself of your #MissionPassion statement everyday
- ✓ Exercise and meditate daily to keep your body fit and mind fresh, to be able to work hard
- ✓ Don't shy to market yourself
- ✓ Ensure that you are learning something new, daily
- ✓ Always keep looking for opportunities to implement your skills

Become a CEO of your career

Now that you are starting on your MissionPassion career journey, you have to become a CEO of your career'. You may ask ", what does that mean? What we have to do?"

What a CEO does? A CEO of a company is accountable for the health of an organization. He always works for the betterment of the company. CEO must have vision where he wants to take the company and should be able to devise the strategies to take the company there. (s)he should work with his team, mentors etc. to prepare a roadmap for the company. CEO must be strong enough to be persistent even if the business is not doing well. He should be always focused on only one goal and that is, company's growth. So now that you are CEO of your career, you must keep focus on only one goal, i.e. your passion career growth. You must become strong, even if you face challenges along the way and should be able to steer your career out of those difficulties and move ahead.

5 Principles for 'Wealth Creation' (Wealth Pyramid™)

I want to congratulate you for starting your journey of '#MissionPassion' and want to wish you a great success. But, only 'Passion' alone won't help if you don't know how to convert your Passion into Wealth. In the Part 2 of this book I am going to explain 5 principles of wealth creation. I don't have any doubt that you will achieve success beyond your dreams, if you follow those principles. These principles have helped all the successful people that you see across the world.

These principles are very easy to follow but they are very effective. You may think if they are easy then why people don't follow them to achieve success? Answer is 'ignorance'. We as elderly people always think that subject of money is complex and it's not for everyone. So, we even don't bother to understand them less implement them. We think that, we need to have 'High IQ' to achieve financial success. But, in fact, subject of money is very straight forward which was made complex.

So, In the 'Part 2' of this book, I have tried to make this subject simple so that everyone can understand and implement it.

Summary

To summarize 'Part 1' of this book, I would like to to urge you to keep your passion alive. Don't let it die for any obstacles or responsibilities. It's your life, it's your passion, so YOU are the one who need to care about it. In fact, if you take good care of your passion, your soul will be happy and it will take care of the rest. I would be happy to hear successful 'MissionPassion' stories from you.

All the very Best for your '#MissionPassion' journey!!!

PART 2

5 Secrets of Wealth

When Sam met Hari

It was a pleasant evening. The cool breeze accentuated the longing for the homeward bound. The birds returning to their nests against the backdrop of the setting sun, intensified the yearning of the old and young alike to return to the warmth of their home. The hustle-bustle of the office dwellers belied the cool evening breeze. Nevertheless, it prompted them to step out of their offices to throng to their favorite Tea Stall for a sip of refreshing tea. It was the most picturesque, pleasant, and peaceful twilight.

This tranquil evening, was, however, marked by severe disruptions in young Sameer's life. An engineering student in his early twenties would remember this day as the one that changed his life. He had envisioned this night as a night to party with his friends and family, having secured his graduation degree. Instead, here he sat, all alone, atop a hill holding a piece of paper that announced him as a failure in life. Hopeless and helpless, he cursed the universe for this conspiracy. Would all the hard work over the years be inconsequential because of one unsuccessful examination result? Emotions ranging from grief, frustration, anxiety, anger, and uncertainty gripped him. His hopes from life had set with the setting sun. He could bear it no longer. Convulsing in unbearable pain, he broke down and succumbed to his feelings. Multiple questions stormed his mind – 'how disappointed would my parents be at this result?', With so much money spent on my education, will I be ever able to secure a job?', 'Future – do I have one anymore?'.

Drowning in the whirlpool of his dismal thoughts, he had resigned to the belief that there was no future for him anymore.

'Dear young man'', he suddenly heard a clear soothing voice cutting through his chaotic thoughts. Sameer looked up. Before he stood a man. Simple but neat attire; fit and fine, muscular physique but the grey in his hair revealed his age. Even though his welled-up eyes, Sameer could sense the calm and serene disposition of this stranger. Happiness radiated from and Sameer could sense it was a reflection of his inner joy.

"Why are you sitting here, all alone and so miserable?", another question.

Sameer wasn't sure he should respond. Though vaguely familiar, try as hard he might, he could not recollect this gentleman's face. He jogged his memory to see if it was anyone of his father's friends. He was sure he would have remembered. And yet. Yet it was a familiar face to him.

"Why are you sitting here, all alone and so miserable?", the old man's resounding voice cut through his thoughts again. Sensing Sameer's dilemma, he continued, "Are you worried about revealing too much to a stranger?" He chuckled, "Let me introduce myself. My name is Hariprasad. I am a businessman, and we have many successful enterprises."

And suddenly things seemed to fall in place! Sameer remembered having researched one of his companies for his project. He recalled reading about Hariprasad in newspapers and magazines. But that was a long time ago. He has read about how he had turned a recluse and away from media glory.

There was no reason for any hesitation now. Sameer narrated his entire tale of woe.

After listening to him, Hariprasad asked 'Now what you are going to do next?" "Not sure, "replied Sameer. "But I don't want to go home and tell my result to parents. They will be angry."

"No, no...don't do that. You must go home and tell this to your parents". They love you and care for you so they may be angry for a while, but they will support you if you tell them your action plan to take care of this result." Said Hariprasad.

"Action plan? What's that and do I need to prepare it?" asked Sameer. I didn't think of anything beyond my exam results apart from applying for a job after my graduation.

"Great!!! That's exactly what most young people do". They don't have any goals or clarity about what they want to achieve in their life. So, most of them follow their parents or relatives because those are the only people they know. Some of them follow their friends' paths and so on. But a handful of them create their path."

"Create my path?" Sameer was now curious. Can one create a new path rather than following one that is tried and tested?".

"Yes, certainly," exclaimed Hariprasad. If one has the courage and conviction, a new path can be created."

"How can I do that?" asked Sameer.

"Before that, let me ask you a question." Why you were upset with your result?" asked Hariprasad.

"Because I failed, Sir! And that too in my final exam with which could have enabled me to secure a job.". Sameer answered with a bit of anger.

"And, why, you want a job?" asked Hariprasad.

"To build a career, earn money and lead a settled life". That's my parents expect from me and they want me to settle down," answered Sameer.

"So, do you think, only a degree result and a job will get you what you are looking for?" asked Hariprasad

"Yes Sir, I think so. I don't know anything else". Sameer replied

"And if you get a job, how much time it will take you to achieve what you want?" Have you thought of it?"

"No, I haven't. As I said, I don't know or haven't been taught to think beyond this." Said Sameer, feeling a little awkward.

"Don't worry, Son! You are not the only one. The majority of kids of your age haven't. And that's why they react like you when they fail or don't get good marks. Some of them even go to extremes like committing suicide, "sighed Hariprasad. "Little do they know what their parents will go through if they take such a drastic step."

It had dawned on Sameer that this was the anchor he was looking for all along. With hope rekindled in his heart, he asked, "Sir, would you guide me? I want to know about other ways to achieve success."

5 Secret Principles of Wealth

"I will! But first tell me, what you are good at?" said Hariprasad. What you love and passionate about?

"I learned many subjects in the school, but I was not good in any of them," said Sameer

"Forget about the school subjects for now. I am asking, "What you love and are good at apart from them?"

"I love cooking and I help my mom in the kitchen many times. Also, I cook for me and my father when my mom is not at home." Sameer answered.

"Good! so, using that skill you can serve at least 50 people in 2 weeks?"

"Serving 50 people in 2 weeks? How that's possible?" asked Sameer

"But you said, you need me to guide you, right?"

"Right", said Sameer

"Good! so, don't ask any more questions. Use your skill and complete the task". Let us meet here again after 2 weeks, same day, same time." Said Hariprasad. "Now, go back home and tell your parents about your result and tell them that you will study hard and pass the exam in the next attempt. Also, tell them that you are undergoing a training that will get you a job. But for that, you must use your kitchen to do some cooking.

Although Sameer didn't understand what and why he is been asked to do but he was now ready to learn to create a new path for himself with the help of his new friend, Hariprasad. Sameer returned home, told his result to his parents, and assured them that he will pass the next exam. He also told his parents about the training and tasks assigned by Hariprasad. His parents were worried about the result, but they were relieved to hear that their son is getting his act together. Sameer had his dinner and went to bed but couldn't sleep since he was thinking of how to complete the task of serving 50 people in 2 weeks.

2 weeks later

Sameer was nervous but also excited. He picked his pace and reached the top of the hill before the decided time. Today's evening brought back memories. It was an evening just like this one and today again he waited anxiously to meet Hariprasad. Hariprasad arrived on time and asked, "Son, were you able to serve 50 people in 2 weeks?"

"No, Sir, replied Sameer feeling guilty. "But I was able to serve 25 people in 2 weeks."

"Good Job, Son. How did you do that?".

Sameer narrated his story. He said," I kept thinking of this task for the whole next day but really couldn't find any idea how to complete this task.

On the same day, my neighbor aunt told me that she wants meals for her old parents for the next 5 days as she is going out of town for some family function. She requested me if I can help her to which I readily agreed. She was happy to hear that. She paid me money in advance for all the meals, even before I could think, whether I should charge and if I can, how much to charge? I was overjoyed to tell my parents that I got my first order to serve homemade meals. They were also happy to hear that.

I was struck by this thought of checking with my neighbors and exploring my neighborhood in search of people who need this service". So, I met neighbors, residents from nearby societies whom I knew, and got a few more orders. I got a few additional orders with the recommendations from my neighbors. I was overjoyed. But now, the challenge was to complete these orders by myself and that too in the time since I need to serve the meals at fixed lunch and dinner time.

I managed to serve 25 customers after doing all the cooking, packing and delivering the meals. Though it was a lot of work and I used to feel tired after the long day, I still got a sense of fulfillment at the end of each day.

While he was narrating his experience, Sameer's excitement was visible on his face. Hariprasad could see the difference this task had brought in Sameer's life. He could see a good change in Sameer as compared to, the one 2 weeks back.

"So, did you understand a different way to achieve the success now?" asked Hariprasad.

No, not really. You said you will teach me that once I complete the task." replied Sameer.

Hariprasad smiled and said, "Young boy, your task was the first secret principle, I want you to understand and practice if you want to achieve success and create great wealth".

"This task was the principle?" asked Sameer with a little surprise.

"Yes, it was. The first principle is, **'serve more and more customers with less and less**'. And I want you to get this carved in your brain, mind and soul, Son! This will help you attain great success.

You know all the famous businesspeople and successful artists, right? They all have followed this principle to create great wealth.

Henry Ford made cars that common people can buy and became successful. Bill Gates developed a computer operating system that the entire world can use and thus became World's richest man. Dhirubhai Ambani built many businesses and the biggest oil refinery to serve people and became highly successful. If you keep focusing on serving yourself by doing a job, your income will be limited but instead, if you aim to serve more and more people you can get returns that you have never imagined. You got what I am saying? So, always remember this. Now, coming back to your task, did you notice, what was your earning after serving 25 customers and whether you could have earned that much in your first month in your job as a new employee?"

Now, Sameer could see the clear picture. He calculated his earnings in the last 2 weeks. He charged around Rs. 150/- per meal for 25 people for 15 days. So, when he calculated, it came to be more than 1 lac rupees (Hundred Thousand). After deducting the cost of raw material etc. he gained a profit of around Rs.75,000/-. Now, this amount was certainly way beyond what he could have earned as a salary from his dream job.

Sameer couldn't believe it and he was overcome with happiness. Hariprasad continued," yes Son, this is just the first principle. If you follow all the 5 principles, you will create wealth beyond your wildest dreams.

"Please tell me, I want to know the remaining principles!" said Sameer with his voice shaking with excitement.

"I will do it, but you need to complete a new task for that."

"A new task? And what is that?" asked Sameer.

"This time, I want you to serve 100 customers in 2 weeks"

Now Sameer was a little worried since he knew how much effort he put in to get those 25 customers and serve them for 2 weeks. And now he needed to do the same for 100 customers.

"How that is possible?" grumbled Sameer.

Hariprasad smiled, patted on Sameer's back, and said, "Think Son, think…!" Let us meet again after 2 weeks at this place at the same time. Hariprasad turned to leave but Sameer kept staring at the retreating figure.

Sameer returned home and told his parents about his success in the last 2 weeks. His parents were also overjoyed to hear that. Sameer also told them about his next goal set by Mr. Hariprasad. Sameer went to bed thinking of the ways to complete his new task.

The next entire day, he kept thinking while he was preparing meals for his customers but was unable to make headway. The next day, one of his friends

called him and said "We have a birthday party at our place the day after tomorrow. Can you please provide us evening snacks for 20–25 guests?" and Sameer jumped with joy on hearing this. He immediately agreed to do this. Though it was difficult to manage everything from preparing, packing, and delivering the food, but he did it happily and successfully. But by now, he was really tired.

He was resting on his favorite chair after completing his day's work when his mother came and said," Son, why don't you ask for help from our house-help? She can help you with cutting vegetables, making chapatis, etc. You can take care of other activities. I can also help to complete the party orders."

"Great idea, mother!", a visibly relaxed Sameer replied. The mere thought of a helping hand allayed his fears.

The next day, Sameer asked, Sudha, their house-help, if she can help him which she readily agreed to. Now, Sameer was able to complete the orders in time and at the same time was able to contact other potential customers. He also approached his existing customers to check if they can give him any party orders. This went on for the next 2 weeks. Sameer was satisfied with his performance. This time, he was able to serve 75 people within 2 weeks. Although it was still short of the target, it gave him a great sense of achievement.

2 weeks later

As agreed, Sameer reached the same place at the same time where Hariprasad was already there waiting for Sameer. He could see the glow on Sameer's face. The glow of achievement and self-confidence.

Hari said, "Looks like, you have completed the task, haven't you?" I could see that on your face.

"I was not able to serve 100 but 75 customers in 2 weeks." Replied Sameer.

"Good, and how did you do that? Last time you could serve only 25 in 2 weeks. What did you do differently this time?" asked Hari.

"I asked for help from our housemaid."

Hari smiled and said," Great, then did you understand the 2nd principle, Son?"

"Nope. I didn't. What is this principle?"

"The second principle is **'using leverage to serve more and more people'**. If you want to achieve greater and bigger goals, you need to use some kind of leverage to share your load." Hari explained. See, you cannot do all the tasks on your own. And even if you try to do that, you will run out of time since you only have 24 hours in a day.

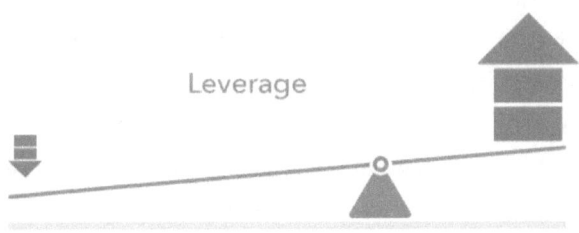

We all have the same 24 hours available at our disposal, but few could get more things done as compared to others in this same time. So, always think of what kind of leverages you can use to achieve bigger goals.

Hari went on," Son, there are many kinds of leverages available. But the 3 most important ones are…

1. Leverage of time (Other Peoples' Time/OPT) – employing people in a factory or restaurant etc.

2. Leverage of money (Other Peoples' Money/OPM) – investing money in the stock market or any business to get a compounding effect or using other people money to build businesses

3. Leverage of information. – build information age business online and earn a fortune

In your case, you used the leverage of time by asking for help and getting those additional hours of effort to complete your task. Now, calculate again how much more you earned this time than your first tasks, just by adding the 'time leverage'.

Leverage of time

This type of leverage is commonly used. All the businesses running around use this type of leverage. Factories, restaurants, offices recruit employees with different skills to work as a team. Here they borrow these employees' time to create a bigger value in the system. Here, employees trade their time with the salary they earn. Here keep in mind that when any businessperson pays any salary to an employee, the employee had earned at least four to five times revenue for the business. This is the reason; businesses grow multiple times than what they are spending. That's why business owners earn more since they get the output of all those hours while employees earn limited and fixed amounts for their own traded hours.

Leverage of money

Let me explain, how one can use the leverage of money. Do you think, business people, use their own money? Do you think, they have all the money they need for any project they plan for? Certainly, No. They use OPM to complete these projects and to create a bigger value than what was originally invested. This way the money is grown in the system. Entrepreneurs and businesspersons borrow loans from banks or other financial institutions which they use to build their business, create value, earn more revenue to pay back the loans with interest to the financial institution. This type of money is called 'debt'. Another type is called 'equity' where investors invest in some businesses to get some percent of the stock of the company. So, when the company grows, its share value grows. You must have heard about angel investors and venture capitalists investing in startups. These people invest their money (leverage money) to create value and create more money. All the banks and financial institutions use this leverage to run their business. Banks take deposits from people at some interest and give loans to businesspeople at higher interest making money for the bank. People invest in the stock market and create more money using this money leverage. There is something known as 'Velocity of Money'. That means how quickly you get returns on the money you invest. So, when you do any business always keep an eye on this because, if the velocity of money is slow, then that indicates, the business model is not effective, and you may have to alter the model or start a new business with a higher velocity of money. E.g. A tea stall owner invests less capital, but he sells a large number of cups to its customers, so the business gives a return on investment quickly and so the business has a higher velocity of money.

Leverage of information & Technology

In today's digital and information age, where information is exchanged every fraction of a second. Smart people are using this information to generate wealth beyond anyone can imagine. In my opinion, this is the best leverage one can use to create enormous wealth. All the giant Silicon Valley companies that we see like Microsoft, Apple, Google, Facebook, Amazon are using information and technology leverage to grow bigger and bigger. At the same time, even smaller companies starting from a small garage (typically knowns as startups) are challenging these giants using the same leverage. So, now, anyone can start an online business and serve any customer in any part of the world. This is true globalization. And the center of all of this is information and technology. This leverage has provided a level playing field for all the players. That's why I said, this is the fastest leverage one can use to create enormous wealth. Those who have information and technology are creating new industries no one has heard of earlier. Social media is the creation of information and technology. Traditional marketing is now taken over by social media marketing and digital marketing. So, with the small budget also, smaller companies can market their products and services across the globe competing with the biggies.

Hari asked, "did you see any improvement in your earnings as compared to last time, with the use of leverage?"

Sameer was surprised to see that he has earned more than double his earlier earnings this time. He was happy.

"Thanks for that, Sir! I understood what you wanted me to learn" said Sameer with curiosity on his face. What's my next task? I want to know the third principle"

Hari was happy that Sameer was learning now and is eager to implement what he is learning.

He said," Now, go back and serve 200 customers but this time you have to serve all kinds of food products to them like breakfast, meals, party orders, birthday cakes, etc. I want you to complete this in 2 weeks.

This time, Sameer was not so worried although he didn't know the answer yet but certainly has gained enough confidence to find a solution along the way.

He bid goodbye to Hari and returned home. He told the entire story and his learnings to his parents. They were very happy to see the positive changes in their son and they thanked the old man.

Now, Sameer was so eager to complete this task he couldn't sleep but just kept on thinking. The next day, he woke up early to plan his day and plan for the next 2 weeks. He was thinking about how he can serve his customers with all the different kinds of meals since even by getting help from Sudha, he may not be to complete the task. He kept thinking and went to the market for some grocery and vegetable shopping. He passed by a cake shop which he knew serves good quality cakes and bakery items. He got an idea and went inside and checked the different cakes and snack items they are offering, their price, etc. He also tried to taste a few of them and bought a few. He also visited a south Indian food stall that serves good quality and tasty breakfast items. He too tasted a few items there and bought a few and returned home. He completed his daily meals serving and then tried the items that he had bought. He found that the products were really good. As per his plan, he could get breakfast, cake, and snack items orders and can outsource them to these 2 vendors. This way, he could serve good quality food to more people and with good margins.

He went back to those 2 vendors and negotiated the price of the items against the assurance of some orders. The vendors were also happy with the deal.

He then printed the pamphlets to advertise his catering services and posted them through the local newspaper delivery person. He too posted the same on social media to get more orders. He was now prepared to serve.

2 weeks passed and he was again at the same corner on the hill, eager to meet his mentor, Hariprasad. This time he had almost achieved his target and was excited to share his experience. Hari came in and Sameer narrated his story. This time he was able to serve almost 200 customers with multiple party orders, birthday cakes, and a combination of breakfast and meal orders.

"Perfect! Said Hari," you have already followed the third principle that I wanted you to learn." The third principle is '*if you want to*

serve more and more, you need to Build Networks'. I hope you must have got it by now. By, outsourcing some of the tasks (by building a network of complementary services around you), you managed to complete the orders and the task. One additional thing you could have done is to add a couple of food delivery people on the assignment basis. This would have helped to offload your delivery load. But anyway, I am happy that you were able to think of the solutions to your problems on your own. This is a very important skill you should build and practice if you want to be a successful businessperson.

This time, you must have already done the calculations of your income, different expenses incurred, and your profit.

Sameer nodded his head in agreement and said, "Yes, this time it was multiple times than the previous one even after all the expenses."

Hariprasad explained," Look Son, building network is very important if you want to grow. Common people look for 'work' while 'successful businesspeople look for 'Network'. You know about McDonald's, right? It is a big network of 'Fast food outlets' across the world. So, the overall power of their network is huge as compared to any stand-alone food joint. Are you getting my point? One cannot do everything in the business world and must get associated with other businesses to grow. So, if you want to be successful, you must focus on building your network and then align it with other big networks. If you observe all the big brands have some network or association with other big networks. This way they both get access to a large customer base. Now, please go home and continue to practice these 3 principles.

"But what about the remaining 2 principles, Sir?" asked Sameer.

"Yes", Hari continued, "Let us meet at our favorite McDonalds on coming Sunday". I will explain the remaining 2 principles while enjoying burgers and fries there.

Sameer smiled and left for his home. He continued to serve his customers, getting new customers, getting new orders that week. But he was now looking forward to Sunday to understand the 2 remaining principles and he was very excited about that.

It was Sunday evening. Sameer hurriedly reached the place. He was waiting for Hari. Hari came in at the agreed time and they both took a table at one corner where they could see the entire restaurant set up.

"How was the week, Son?" asked Hari. "It was good, Sir. Added few more customers", replied Sameer.

"Good! What you would like to order?" asked Hari.

"I would go with a Veg Burger", said Sameer.

"Get me a too a veg burger and coffee, Son." Said Hari.

Sameer went to the order taking counter where he was greeted by the counter person.

The counter person took the order and asked Sameer if he would like to add medium fries and a drink to his burger order with some additional amount. Sameer agreed and returned with the food on the table.

Looking at his tray, Hari asked, "But you ordered only Burger, right?"

"Yes, but the counter person asked me if I would like to upgrade it to a meal by adding some fries and a drink with little additional money. So, I accepted that offer," replied Sameer.

"Perfect!" exclaimed Hari. Enjoy your food.

"What is the 4th principle, Sir?" Hari asked impatiently.

"The one that you just learned, Sameer," smiled Hari.

"Which one? You didn't say anything about any principle. Sameer didn't get what Hari was saying.

"Look son, who took the order from you? You asked for a burger but ended up with a burger, fries, and a drink, right?". This is known as cross-selling. Cross-selling means selling some add on products with not much additional cost so that even customer doesn't mind buying it. Upselling means, selling advanced or better product version with little extra amount. In this way, the counter person added to the daily sales numbers. Did you get it now?" Imagine, this same cross-selling and upselling happens across thousands of McDonald's outlets across the world making it a richer and successful business. Do you remember, when I asked you to serve your customers all types of meals right from breakfast, meals, snacks, and party orders? That was a kind of cross-selling and upselling. You can increase your revenue by selling different products or services to your existing customers at a lower price. This is beneficial for you since you don't have to spend time and money to acquire a new customer and at the same time, your customer gets a good product and service at a lesser cost. Now, do you remember that boy, who took your order? Was he the owner of McDonald's?" Of course not. He was not even the owner of this Franchised outlet. Then why he was bothered to sell more to customers. Did you see the owner preparing the burger patty behind the counter? You got, what I am saying. McDonald's is a *'Business System'* that is run by employees at various levels. They follow the exact defined processes to serve the food quickly to thousands of customers across the globe. So, the 4th principle is **'to serve more and more people, you need to build 'Business Systems'.**

Here, can you also see how different processes are working synchronously like order-taking process, cooking process, inventory stocking, raising funds, signing franchisee contracts, etc. work together for McDonald's' brand. Like this, all the businesses that exist across the globe, more or less have similar kinds of systems, so the brands get bigger and famous. So, if you want to build a strong business, you need to have a business system to run it. Of course, it's not going to happen overnight, and it takes a lot of resources to build one. But, if you know the fundamentals of what a business system is, you can certainly start building one day at a time.

Hari further explained, "there are 3 types of Business Systems.

    a. Incorporating (Limited companies)

    b. Franchising

    c. Direct Selling (Network Marketing)

a. Incorporating (Limited companies)

The various types of limited companies come under this system.

One can form a proprietorship, partnership, private limited, and public limited company within this business system. Proprietorship is the simple one where the owner is the business where the owner is accountable for the profit or loss of the business. In Private limited companies, the liability of the owner is limited to some percentage. In, partnership type, the liability of the partners is defined in the partnership agreement. Public limited companies are the ones that get listed on the stock exchanges and thousands of stockholders are owners of the business. This system is a typical business system and has various rules and regulations. This helps to build a strong business foundation for big organizations. All the biggies that you see around are mostly of this type.

Advantages

- ✓ Robust business system
- ✓ More control over the system

Disadvantages

- High capital required
- Expansion becomes difficult and slow

b. Franchising

World-famous fast food brands like McDonald's, Subway, Dominos are of this type. In this system, a company builds and establishes a brand, product/services, processes, and then it gives rights to other people to create the same setup with the same brand name. The parent company is called 'Franchisor' and the one taking the rights is called a 'Franchisee'. Franchisor typically charges a one-time fee known as 'Franchise fee' to the franchisee. Franchisee gets the entire ready business model to start with. Franchisee also must give some royalty to the Franchisor for ongoing support, as a contribution to the advertising and using the brand name. The following points need to be checked related to the Franchisor company before buying a franchise...

- Investment – This is in the form of
    - Franchisee fee
    - Royalty
    - Advertising Fee
- Brand name in the market
- Freedom in the system – Typically Franchisor wants to keep all thing standardized in terms of space, interior, items to be sold, operating processes, geographical area to sell,

etc. All these things to be checked before going ahead with the investment

- Standardization of processes
- Training and support from the Franchisor
- The legality of the Franchisor
- Franchisee contract cancellation and renewal terms

Also, before going with buying a Franchisee, one needs to do some self-assessment based on these points...

- Your investment capacity
- Your skills
- Your financial objectives/goals

Once done with this assessment, you need to do some research related to the product/services that you are going to sell...

- Demand for the products
- Competition
- Products range and market size

After checking all the above points, one can take a final decision to buy a franchisee.

Advantages

- ✓ Less capital investment for expansion
- ✓ The fast expansion of business
- ✓ Quick global expansion with lesser resources
- ✓ Regular cash flow in the form of royalty
- ✓ Benefits of existing brand name for the franchisee

Disadvantages

- Monitoring and control not easy
- The franchisee cannot add any products/services without approval from the franchisor
- A lot of dependency on franchisees
- Difficult to introduce newer products in the market

Direct Selling

Now let me tell you something about 'Direct Selling'. This system is new as compared to the other two. This system is more suitable for common people who want to start something on their own.

As the name suggests, the system helps to sell the products and services of a company. Instead of following the traditional sales and distribution (S&D) channel of product advertisement, appointing stockiest, distributors, and retailers, the company gives commission to its customers who perform all the roles of doing advertising, distributor, and retailer. This helps the customer to get the product at a lesser cost and in turn, gets a commission for 'selling products directly' to other customers whom they know (within their network). These distributors can also build a team of similar distributors and build a network of distributors. So, this system is also called 'Network Marketing'. This way, the distributor who builds the network gets some commission from the sales done in the network. The company provides required training about products and selling skills to the direct sellers so that they can sell the products efficiently and effectively. Thus, the system trains the common people to become efficient salespeople. This is very important since 'selling' is the most important skill an Entrepreneur and Businessperson can have. As well-known Financial Literacy Guru, Mr. Robert Kiyosaki said, "if you can sell, you don't need a job. "This way the direct seller can become a businessperson without bothering about other business complexities. So, in my opinion, one who wants to become an Entrepreneur should practice selling, by becoming a direct seller first.

Direct selling had helped thousands of wannabe entrepreneurs to start their own business in their spare time and take advantage of all the principles of leverage, network, and business system without worrying about managing the overheads that other types of business system owners had to manage. So, this system is the best with more advantages than disadvantages. But unfortunately, this system had received a bad reputation because of the ill practices followed by many companies and direct sellers. Ponzi investment schemes giving false promises to double your income etc. have damaged the reputation of this beautiful system. In this system, the key thing is the product or service that is being sold and for which direct sellers get the commission. But, misunderstanding this system as 'make quick money' scheme, many companies and leaders mislead people to focus more on the commissions thus losing focus on the products, resulting in frauds, scams and creating a bad reputation for the overall system.

So, in my opinion, if this system is followed and executed in its pure form, is the best system we ever had designed.

Now, let us see some of the points that one must check before entering direct selling.

- ✓ Self-Image – Before starting with selling any products/services just check if that product is not going to affect your image in society. E.g. if a well-respected person joins a company to sell not so reputed products, it may harm his self-image in society.

- ✓ Efforts against Returns – One must check the amount of effort that one needs to put against the returns. If the efforts are more against the returns, then it's not advisable to start with that company

- ✓ Investment – This is very important to check what is the total investment to be made to start this. If the investment is too high then, one can find something with a lower one elsewhere.

- ✓ Legality – Before starting with direct selling for any company, one needs to check all the legal things for the company. Later these things can hamper your business and social image as well

- ✓ Need – This may be perhaps the most important point since if there is no enough need for the product/service in the market, there is no point in starting with this company

- ✓ Training – As mentioned earlier, one of the main advantages of getting into direct selling is the training that one gets from the company in the form of product and sales training. So, choose a company that has a good training program.

Once done with the research and started with Direct selling, one should follow these points to achieve success in the business…

- Set your financial goal and create a plan to achieve it – You must set clear financial goals as to how much returns you want from this business and how much time and energy you are going to put in. Because, if you don't have this clarity then you will just work but won't get good results.

- Make a list of prospects – As we saw earlier, this business is based on the products shared and sold to the people we know. So, one must prepare a list of prospective consumers within his/her family, friends, colleagues, etc. Since these are the people who are likely to trust you the chances of making a sale are high. This will boost your self-confidence and confidence in the product and system.

- Get training – This is very important to get yourself trained on the products and sales to be confident when you recommend someone about the products

- Build confidence – You need to tell confidently about the products and your business. Unless you show that confidence, your customers won't get that, and you won't be able to close a sale.

- Doing a follow-up – one should not expect all the prospects will buy from you immediately. So, you must keep patience and do follow-ups to close the sale.

- Following your leaders and helping your team – This is also known as 'Duplication'. You have to just duplicate what your seniors (upline) have done and also ask your juniors (downline) to do what you are doing. Since this is a team business, you must work collaboratively. If you work together, you will achieve success.

- Keep patience and persistence – This business is not an 'overnight success' or 'make rich quick' business. If someone tells you so, it's a complete lie. This business, like any other business, takes efforts and time. This needs to be built one day at a time. So, keep patience and work persistently to achieve success.

Advantages

- ✓ Little or no capital required to start a business
- ✓ Effective training for overall personal growth
- ✓ One can focus on just selling without bothering about other business complexities
- ✓ One gets the benefit of a trusted and established brand

Disadvantages

- No control over product/services quality
- The bad reputation of 'Direct Selling' in the market

Sameer was now very clear why some businesses remain small; some grow a little but never cross certain geographical areas while some grow very big and run across the world.

Hari continued, "the business systems that I mentioned, are the main ones and anyone can design and build a one using the framework of any of those 3 systems. Once you start working more and start getting experience, you can think of which system is best suited for you and your business. The beauty of building a business system is it works even if you are not around. Again, a good example is McDonald's. Even if its founder is no more now, the system is running successfully for years and will continue for years to come. To understand the business system better, let me tell you a story that I read in a book. It will help you to internalize the concept of the business system and its benefits for the rest of your life.

Sameer was now eager to hear the story. He was considering himself lucky to get a mentor like Hari and thanked God for letting him face the failure in the exams. He said eagerly, "yeah, I would love to hear the story'

Hari started," once upon a time, there was a village. Far away from the village, there was a lake from which people used to bring water for their daily needs. It was very time consuming for them to spend hours to bring the water. So, they decided to give the job of filling the water to 2 people Sachin and Sandeep. Their job was to fill water from this lake into a tank in the village on daily basis. They were paid per bucket of water they fill throughout the day. Since Sachin and Sandeep were jobless at that time they happily agreed to take up this tedious job.

They started their work. They both used to start early morning and work for 8 to 9 hours filling up the buckets, carrying it, and emptying them into this tank. Days passed and Sachin started feeling bored with this work. He also started getting back pain. Sandeep also had similar issues but both continued.

After long hours of working they both used to sit for some time and discuss the job and the issues, they are facing. But still, they didn't have any solution, so they continued. Sachin was always thinking of how he can solve this problem. So, after finishing his daily work, he used to read, think of the possible solutions. One day, he got an idea and he called his friend to share the idea with him. Sachin said," Sandeep, I think, I have an idea that will solve our issues and we don't have to fill the buckets on daily basis. We can construct and lay a pipeline from the lake to the tank and fit a tap on both sides. This way, water will flow from the lake whenever we want, and we don't have to work again. We can charge the villagers some money per bucket they take from the tank." But Sandeep was not so impressed with this idea. He said," Sachin, what is a pipeline? Do you know how to construct this? And if we construct this, it will eat up some of our daily working hours and we will get less money per day. So, we won't be able to earn enough to buy for our daily needs. We may also lose our job because we won't be able to work with our full capacity. So, I am not joining you with this idea. If you want, you can go ahead.

But Sachin didn't give up. He was determined to work on his idea and was ready to make some sacrifices. He declared to the villagers that he will be working for 4 hours daily and his friend Sandeep will get his son to help him to work with him for the remaining 4 hours. So, Sandeep started getting more money per day and was happy. He was earning more than Sachin and was able to buy good things to keep his family happy. At the same time, Sachin was now spending his more time to construct the pipeline. His daily earning was less so he had to reduce his spending. But he was ready and was sure that his efforts will pay him in the long run.

Weeks passed, and Sachin's pipeline was halfway ready from the lake. He continued to work on it. In another 2 months, he was ready with his pipeline. He tested if the pipeline is working fine or not. He started the tap from the lake end and the water flowed through the pipeline into the tank in few seconds. The water was pure, clean with no dirt in it. He was very happy to see his dream fulfilled.

He called up the villagers to show them his pipeline working. They were also happy to see the quality of water and to see that they don't have to wait till evening to get the water like earlier.

Also, the money per bucket was lesser than what Sachin and Sandeep charging earlier. So, they agreed to pay Sachin per bucket. Now, every day Sachin just had to put on the tap and collect the money from the villagers at the tank end.

He was able to earn more money even he was not present on the daily basis. On the other hand, Sandeep lost his job since his services were no more needed with the pipeline giving better quality water conveniently. He was upset and went to Sachin to complain. Sachin said," I asked you to join me when I started this project, but you rejected it and now you are suffering and complaining. This is not good." He continued," Sandeep, I can understand your problem and frustration and I want to offer this same opportunity to you once again. I am working on a similar project for other villages as well where I need good partners and I want you to be my partner. Are you ready, now?" Sandeep was overjoyed and readily agreed. They together worked on many such pipelines project and created tremendous wealth. Wherever they go, they see people filling buckets and are frustrated but still not doing anything about it. Even if Sachin and Sandeep offer them the opportunity they are not ready to grab it because of fear and lack of knowledge.

Saying this Hari ended the story and asked," Son, did you understand what is meant by 'filling buckets and building a pipeline' in the story?"

"Yes, I got it." Replied Sameer. Filling buckets is like doing a job or self-employment and building a pipeline means building business systems.

"Dart on!" Said Hari with a smile. He was happy to see that Sameer has learned his lessons well. Yes, Son, there are always different ways to do things, it's just how do you see things. And this is the last and the most important principle. This principle is about the 'Mindset'. **If you want to be successful in business, you must have the mindset of a business person**. Your mind should focus on the 'solution' and not just worrying and crying about the 'problem'. If you look for problems, you will see problems but if you are focused on finding solutions, you will find solutions. This is how nature works. Our brain is programmed accordingly. If you give someone the task of finding only Honda cars from the crowd, our brain will only find Honda cars. Similarly, if you are looking for some job vacancies in the newspaper you will see only 'job vacancies' and nothing else. In the same way, if you want to become a successful businessperson, then you need to train your brain to see 'business opportunities' everywhere and every time. There are only two sides you can be on. One is the problem side and the other is the solution side. So, if you are not a part of the solution then you are part of the problem and that won't lead you to success. Always remember, "Losers give reasons and leaders give results". I want you to be a leader. And the big quality of a leader is to take risks. You see many people in this world are educated and intellectuals but not necessarily are successful. It's mostly because of their mental conditioning.

They are not taught to take risks and in fact, taught to play safe. From our school days, we are conditioned not to take risks and always play it safe. We are punished to make mistakes but in real life that's not how we learn. We learn to walk after a few failed attempts. We learn to ride a bicycle after falling a few times. In the business world too, you need to take some risks and learn from the mistakes to be better the next time. But people always find easy ways to do things so to earn money also, they choose the easiest way to trade their time for money thus end up taking up a job. But they forget that time is limited, and money is infinite. So, always remember to use 'time leverage' to create wealth beyond our limits.

But don't misunderstand that I am saying that you must earn lots of wealth to consider yourself successful. I will never ask you to do that. Some wealthy people get so obsessed with the money and wealth that they forget to 'live'. All I am saying that you need to take control of the money and not let money take charge of your life. Remember, humans have created money, not the other way around. Now, let me tell you something about money.

"About money?" asked Sam thinking what different thing Hari is going to tell about money that he is not aware of.

Something about 'Money'

Hari asked, "What is money? Is it gold, is it currency, is it bank balance? Is it stocks? Is it the real estate that we own? What is it exactly? It is everything that we saw above but at the same time, it is not real. It is, what you agree it is. In pure terms, money is just a medium to represent 'value' to complete any transaction. That means, when any transaction happens it happens between the exchange of two values. Money is just a representation of that value. In earlier days, when there was no money (currency), transactions used to happen by exchanging products only. It is known as the 'Barter System'. Over the years, for the need for some convenient medium of transaction, the currency was introduced. But unfortunately, this medium is now considered as a 'product' and everyone wants to 'own' and 'hold' this product. Because of this, the money is held by people and thus not circulated well in the economy thus creating issues of uneven distribution of money. Hari continued, "Son, always try to understand the things at its core without getting into its complexities. People who design the policies and systems and those who run the financial world have made 'money' a complex subject so that the common person would find it difficult to understand and they can rule you. This will help them to play with that money easily and common people will always remain ignorant and will do what these policymakers want them to do. Our tax system and other systems are made so complex that a common person cannot understand it easily. So, so-called financial gurus get benefitted from this. So, if you want to become successful, you need to understand the fundamentals of money so that you can use it to your advantage. Always remember that "*there is infinite money available in the world and market, it's just that, how much you can access and use to create more (value) in the society.* Rich and successful business people know that money is a byproduct that we get for creating value. So, they focus on creating value and not on the money. They get money as a byproduct which they again invest to create value. So, always, keep in mind that if you chase money, it will run away from you but if you aim at creating value and serving people, then the money will start following you.

Work with Passion

Hari continued," Son, mindset is very important when it comes to doing anything worthwhile. And when I say mindset, a big part is 'having a passion for what you do'. Remember, what

I asked you the first time before giving you a task to serve 50 people in 2 weeks. I asked you," what you love and what you are good at?" What I wanted to check was, what you are passionate about? Because even if you have tried to complete the task using any of the subjects or skills that you had acquired it would not have given you the work satisfaction and sense of achievement. Passion plays a very big role in our success. When we do what we love, that is when we work on what we are passionate about, our body and soul work together to ensure we get success. Even if we face some failures initially, passion helps us to keep going and to focus on what you are set to do. And that's why even though you couldn't complete your tasks fully for the first few times, it didn't discourage you because your soul was sure that one day you will be able to make it. You failed in the exams which may be because you didn't like the subjects and it was not your strength. The main problem with our education system is that 'it asks us to put more effort into the subjects that we are weak in'. The issue with that is, 'the subject that we are weak in' eats up our time, energy and focus that we could have given to further develop the subject that we are good at'. But since the entire system is designed around getting a certificate by learning all the subjects even though students may or may not have any interest in some of them. So, the system is designed to 'get us a job' and not 'make us learn'. This is the key reason; we are seeing so many students are not getting jobs even after completing their education. If we dig further into this problem, we will find that students have 'passed the exams' but haven't really 'understood' the subjects. This is because they didn't have an 'interest' in those subjects. Their soul and heart were not there. You got what I am saying. In short, our system is focused on creating 'certified educated' people but have simply ignored to create 'knowledgeable Skilled' people. And that's why we are seeing a heavy shortage of 'skilled' people around.

80/20 principle

Sam, there is a famous principle named 80/20, given by a mathematician, Alfred Pareto. It says that generally 80% of the work is done by 20% of the people. One gets 80% of the result by focusing on 20% tasks and so on. You must always remember this principle and apply it anywhere you want to achieve something. Your 20% efforts will give 80% results, 20% of the products will get you 80% of the revenue, 20% of the customers will fetch you 80% of the sales, and so on. So, whatever you do, please apply this principle to help you focus on the right things.

Be-Do-Have principle

"Let's move now from here and take a walk", said Hari. So, they got up and headed towards the nearest walkway. Hari said," Sam, there is something important to learn to understand the principle of 'mindset'.

"What it is?" asked Sameer.

"It is called the 'Be-Do-Have' principle. You see, people set goals now and then. There is a fashion to set 'New Year resolution'. But, do you know why most of these resolutions didn't get fulfilled? People set goals and to achieve those goals they plan for certain tasks or activities to complete. They start with enthusiasm but over time that enthusiasm fades away and they fall off from that path to reach the goal. It is because they focus on 'Have' i.e. goal and 'Do' the tasks, but they generally forget to 'Be' and that means they don't make up their mind on the goal. They don't internalize that goal and they fail. So, it is very important to work on your mindset first before following other principles if you want to have long term benefits. Remember, when we met for the first time, I didn't give you a solution but instead, made you think of the solution so that your mind can help find your solutions for your problems. In schools and at home, teachers and parents typically try to provide answers and solutions to our problems, and that, in a way, makes us dependent on others for the solutions. Ideally, we should learn to find our ways to tackle the problems. If you see, elders limit their children by saying that their children should study hard to get a good job and settle. On the contrary, they miss seeing that their child may have the ability to attain much higher goals, but they force their limits on their child. E.g. a child may have the capacity to become a Dhirubhai or a Steve Jobs but elders may limit that child to become a bank officer or something similar because they cannot think beyond that and thinks that's the greatest thing their child can achieve.

The first step of Learning is Unlearning

Hari went on and said," Sam, we all are learning all the time. But unfortunately, people consider 'our formal education' as 'Learning' and so they stop learning after they get a certificate or a degree. So, when you enter the real world of business and job, the first step of learning is *Unlearning* some of what you have learned so far. Because your classroom education is far different than what you face when you enter the streets. So, you need to be more agile and adaptive to learn new things quickly and implement it as you move on. People are so rigid with their degree or certificate that they don't like to learn something new and adapt to a change and most of the time they fail because of not able to cope up with this change. You see, change is the only constant in this world, and in this information and digital era, changes are very rapid. Even the, once bigger companies, washed off because they were not able to adapt to the new world. Many careers and jobs became obsolete. But, if you are always focused on 'creating a value', you will not only be able to survive but also will be able to succeed in the everchanging environment around. Also, one important quality is to challenge the status quo. Because if you continue to do what you are currently doing, you will continue to get what you are currently getting. So, you must do things differently if you want different and better results than the existing ones. This helps you to make progress. All the inventions happened following this one single principle.

Saying this Hari stopped and said," Son, I think, you have learned 5 principles well and now it's the time to practice them. Now, go back and have a look at your current business and see how you can make changes or additions to it to improve it. Sam thanked Hari for his advice and returned home.

Sam grows the Business

Sam continued his business for a year or so from his home. He used to call Hari in between but now they were not meeting frequently as Sam got busy in his business. He took up a bank loan and put some of his own money to rent a space to set up a kitchen from where he can serve his customers. He bought good equipment and hired a few qualified cooks with no working experience to help him. Now because of this new well-equipped place, he was able to serve more customers.

He designed the processes and standardized all the recipes so that the cooks can follow the same to prepare the food with the same quality and same taste every time. Also, he trained the order taking staff to take up the orders that come on the phone or social media app. This way, he could focus on planning, strategizing, and getting new business rather than getting completely involved in daily operations. He was now spending a few hours in the kitchen and the rest he was spending in networking, establishing business relations with vendors, etc. His business was growing day by day.

In the first year, Sam was operating from his home. In the second year, he built his kitchen. Now, he was thinking that he can expand this further by involving some partners who are passionate about food, who want to start something on their own and can invest some money and time. He designed a partnership model where he would prepare all the food and partners just had to take and deliver the orders to customers. Also, there are many retail products that he had developed which can be put up at partners' location and can be sold by partners with a good commission. He was asking for very little investment from the partners, so he received many inquiries. He signed up many such partners and his brand grew.

Within six months, he had around 20 partners and his turnover increased 3–4 times than what he had with a single kitchen. He hired an experienced cook who he knew through one of his contacts to manage the daily operations. He also hired a 'Business Development Manager' named 'Raj, who can look after the partners. Sam just focused more on business development and adding new recipes and products. He was also encouraging his staff to come up with new ideas of doing things differently. They were also motivated to work from their head, heart, and soul because they are getting good money, good experience, and more importantly, they are getting a feeling that their voice and ideas are heard and implemented. His business kept growing for the next couple of years. He used to meet Hari, once or twice a year to give him updates about the business progress and seek his guidance to develop strategies for business growth. Hari was very happy with Sam's progress.

Venturing into a Niche

All this while, Sam was thinking, what he is currently doing is what many other businesses are also doing. Although the market is big where he had established a good brand name for his services and had gained a good customer loyalty, he was now thinking to create a niche for his business. Sam wanted to follow the 'Blue Ocean' strategy, that Hari had taught him. Blue Ocean Strategy is to create a separate market (ocean refers to market) for yourself rather than fighting or competing in the already crowded market and get eaten up by sharks (refer to 'Red Ocean').

He was reading and researching deciding the niche. Sam was thinking about what he would love to work on next and most importantly, what customers need. While doing the research and looking at the feedback from his customers, he observed that the customers are looking for healthy food options within his current meal services. Sam further analyzed this and found that many people have some food restrictions, some are on diet, few want to go for weight loss or weight gain program, etc. and want the food to suit their needs. "This is a good market to tap", said Sam to himself. He also shared his thoughts with his team and of course with Hari. Everyone agreed that they should go for this opportunity. Hari suggested that Sam should hire or partner with a Nutritionist to design the authentic recipes and to provide Nutrition Consultancy to his customers. Sam was now ready to plunge into this new domain with his team's support.

Entering a Niche - Serving Healthy Food

As suggested by Hari, Sam searched for a Nutritionist who would love to join him. As Hari had taught Sam, that one should not go for a partner without any financial stake from the partner. Because if there is no financial stake, people generally don't get serious about the business or don't put their 100% in it because they have nothing to lose if things don't go as planned and expected. Also, Sam was not going to go for someone who wants to do this part-time because Hari had said to him that there is nothing like a part-time job in this world. The problem with part-time work is that the person doing it, cannot focus on both the jobs and as a result, no job is done effectively. Also, when someone wants to do something part-time means that person is not confident about his/her main job and not about part-time work either. So, in short, no job is done well. So, Sam was looking for someone who either would join on salary and with some stake as well. And, more importantly, the one who shares his vision to build a 'Health Hub' across the country. He floated an ad on the recruitment site and social media asking for interested people to join him. He received many applications. Sam was not in a hurry to recruit because he wanted to make sure he is making a good choice by evaluating the person well. He interviewed almost 10–20 candidates before finalizing one. Sam was happy that he had got a perfect person to add the complementary skillset to the team. Her name was Sia. She not only had a good experience as a Nutritionist but also had an entrepreneurial spirit that Sam was looking for. Sia too was looking for such an opportunity, so it was a perfect match.

Healthy food Niche Journey

Sia joined Sam in a month after finishing her earlier job commitments. Before even she joined, she started working on designing the menu and nutrition packages that they had decided to start serving in their new venture. She started having meetings with Sam to show him the menu items and various packages that she had designed. Sam and Sia spent a lot of time to fine-tune their offerings. After a few days, they finalized the menu, it's design and pricing, etc. After Sia joined, she conducted the trials for the designed menu to fine-tune the recipe. The next key task was to get funding for the new venture.

Raising Finance

Sam asked Sia to calculate the budget and create financial projections for the scope of services she was planning for. She came up with the overall business plan. Now it was Sam's turn to find good financers to fund this. He approached a few investors as referenced by Hari earlier. After spending so much time with Hari, Sam had now learned to prepare good business plans and vision story to pitch to the investors. He and Sia put up the vision to create a 'Health Hub' for the investors. After presenting around

20–30 investors and many rounds of discussions, 2 investors agreed to provide the required amount for the new venture. Sam called Hari to update him about this. Hari said, "Good!!! Son. Ready to build your second pipeline?" Sam smiled and replied, "Yes, very much."

Execution began...

Sia took the responsibility and ownership of branding and promotion. She planned to connect with the existing customers who were asking for healthy food options. Those were the easy customers to acquire and to get feedback from, for the new menu. She started giving some samples to those customers and asked for their suggestions. The initial response was good, and she got positive feedback and received a few suggestions to do some changes. She shared all this with Sam and discussed with him about the launching of this venture. Sam was excited to hear all this and eager to launch it as soon as possible. Sia started taking free 'Health and Nutrition' sessions in the afternoon time when typically, the housewives have some free time after sending their kids to school. Sia got the ad for these sessions published on social media asking interested people to pre-book for the sessions. She got an overwhelming response.

She started taking sessions and giving free samples of the products that she had developed to get feedback. As learned from Hari, Sam was looking for a more subscription-based business to get ensured business and good cash flow. Sia, asked Sam," What are other Revenue models that businesses can use?". Sam said, "what I learned from Hari and my reads, there are 3 other models apart from 'Subscriptions'. They are…

- o Freemium
- o One-time fee
- o Affiliate/advertising/referral

In the 'Freemium' model, which is a combination of 'Free and Premium', the base product is Free to get more customers in but if anyone wants an advanced product with more features, they have to pay'. A lot of internet-based products follow this model.

In the one-time fee model, customers are charged with a one-time fee for a long period of service. Generally, the service industry adopts this model where they sign a 'service contract' with the customers for 3 or 5 years, to provide post-warranty support.

In the Affiliate/advertising/referral model, business/people get some commissions, if the sale is made after they promote products and services of other businesses. This model is good for businesses who have a good customer following. This model can help businesses to get good revenue just by leveraging their existing customer base.

Also, there is a 4th model and that is an 'Aggregator' model. In this model, a business builds a platform where other businesses can sell their products and services. Well-known examples are Amazon, Flipkart, Make my Trip, etc. In turn, they earn good revenue by charging some percentage of each sale made from their platform."

Sam said further, "Businesses can adopt one or more revenue models, depending on their business type. We too will add some of these models in the future along with the subscription model". Sia thanked Sam as she had learned something new today. Sam and Sia designed few subscription plans and started communicating the same with their existing customers and during the Nutrition sessions that Sia was conducting. Sia also had a plan to add an 'end to end' Nutrition Consultancy service to the customers. This means clients will get Nutrition consultation and the recommended food and supplements through their venture so that clients don't have to worry about where to get the recommended food from. It was a win-win for everyone since clients will get the required things easily and at a value price and at the same time, Business will get customer loyalty. Sam was happy to hear about this 'end to end' plan because it was in line with his vision of making his new venture a 'Health-Hub'. So, he readily approved the proposal and Sia started working on it.

Launching the Niche services

Sam launched the new venture from the new place nearby from his earlier place. He planned for both the places nearby so that he and other members can easily move between the two kitchens depending on the workload. Because of all the efforts, Sia put in, they got several subscriptions to begin with. Also, Sia started conducting the nutrition sessions which also received a good response from the customers. Soon, their new venture got good momentum and within six months, Sam was able to double his customer base. Sia also became a known person among the customers with her expertise and excellent customer service skills. After the first year of operations, Sam and Sia's venture was already making half the revenue that Sam's first venture was making. But Sam had not lost his focus on his first pipeline and kept on adding new partners with the help of Raj, who was now looking after the business development as well. Now that the new venture was stable and reached the breakeven level of the initial investment, Sam started thinking about the next step.

Building a Health Hub

Sam discussed, his idea of creating a 'Health Hub' with Sia and Raj. Sam had recently read about 'Business Model Canvas' designed by Alexander Osterwalder and Yves Pigneur which can help them to understand and develop their new business model.

Sam said," guys, let us use the 'Business Model Canvas' to build our business model. "What is it?" asked Raj. Sam started explaining," Business Model Canvas (BMC) is a strategic tool used for visually developing or displaying a business model. A BMC helps determine and align the key business activities and their relationship to your value proposition. The Business Model Canvas contains nine blocks as shown in this diagram. Each block represents a business element constituting a business.

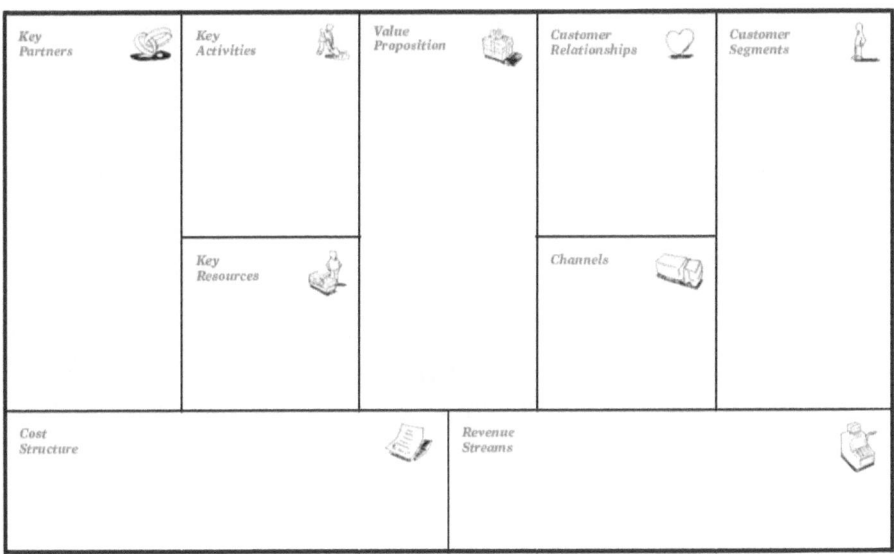

The 9 elements of a business model canvas are...

1. Key partners: We need to list the key partnerships our business leverages or relies upon for success. We must Include the resources or value your business gets from these partnerships.

2. Key activities: Here we can summarize the key activities that allow our business to provide services and deliver on our value proposition.

3. Key resources: We will list the key resources our business relies upon or uses to operate and provide services.

4. Key propositions: This is the block where we need to summarize the different value propositions that set our business apart from the competition.

5. Customer relationships: Here, we can define and describe the primary relationships we have with our customers, including how we interact with them, how these interactions differ among different types of customers, and the level of support the different customers receive.

6. Channels: This block helps us to detail how our customers are reached, how our services are provided, our different distribution channels, and how our value proposition is delivered.

7. Customer segments: We need to define the ideal customer personas our value proposition is intended to benefit, then describe the key differences between these segments.

8. Cost structure: Here, we will identify the primary costs associated with operating our business and providing our

services, then detail the relationship between these costs and other business functions.

9. Revenue streams: This is where we will describe how our business generates revenue through the delivery of our value proposition.

Sam continued," we can fill these 9 blocks for our business to get more clarity of our business model. We can fill in each block using stickies, hand drawings, pictures etc.to detail each business element. If you observe, the left part of the Canvas is about the business elements that are used (Inputs) to create value for the customers and the right side of the canvas is to define the customer and value that a business plan to create for its customers (Output)."

They all brainstormed together and completed the Business Canvas for the 'Health Hub' business that they are going to build. They spent 2 days on this planning but now they had more clarity about what their business model will look like and what they want to do to grow it. They are set and ready to take a plunge now.

Building the Health Hub

When Sam started with his niche venture to serve healthy food to its customers, his vision was to eventually create a health hub. This hub will provide all the products and services related to health to its customers under one roof. Clients will get everything, right from the Nutrition Consultation to the healthy products, supplements, and other services related to 'Health and Wellness', like Yoga, meditation, etc. But his plan was not to reinvent the wheel himself but to create an ecosystem or a platform where even other products and service providers who have good and unique products and services to offer can help him serve his customers. He wanted to follow the first principle (To serve more and more customers) that his mentor had taught him. But he also didn't want to miss on the second principle (use leverage of time and money) and the third principle (build the network) as well. He wanted to build a strong business system (fourth principle) using all the principles that he had learned and practiced so far. Now, with Sia and Raj around and guidance from his friend, Hari, he was ready to fulfill his vision.

Sam, Raj, and Sia distributed ownership of various work areas and tasks that they must take care of, for the 'Health Hub'. Sam was responsible for the overall growth and took ownership of adding Business Partners and Vendors tie-ups while Raj took up Marketing and Customer management. Sia was going to take care of product R&D and Operations. They finalized the staff and resource requirements for their respective departments and the funding required. They decided to go initially for debt capital and then subsequently for equity at a later stage. They had a plan to set up the first hub themselves and then add 'Business Partners' in different cities and districts. This way, Sam was following the 'Money Leverage' (OPM-Other People's Money) principle to grow his brand and business. Sam, called Hari since he was very excited to share all these updates with him. They agreed to meet at their favorite place, on the hill at sunset time.

Bid Goodbye!

It was evening and the sun was about to set. Sam was eager to meet Hari to tell him about 'Health Hub' plans. He was waiting for Hari. Generally, Hari is never late for meetings, so Sam was a little surprised. He thought maybe Hari has stuck up in traffic but then he didn't call to inform that he is getting late. Sam waited for a while, but Hari didn't turn up. Sam tried calling him, but the phone was not reachable. Sam was sad as he was not able to share this big update with his mentor, his dear friend, his philosopher. He returned home. The next day, in the morning, his doorbell rang. Sam opened the door and saw a courier company boy. There was an envelope for him. He received the envelope and was surprised to see a letter. "Who must have sent this letter?" he asked himself. Because these days people send emails. He opened the letter and was overjoyed to see that it was from, Hari. Sam started reading the letter. As he went on reading, his eyes filled with tears. He couldn't believe what he was reading. The letter read like this...

Dear Sam,

I am happy to see your progress, and this shows that you have understood the principles of wealth creation, I wanted you to learn. And I am sure that you will continue to follow them throughout your career journey.

You must be surprised and upset about why I didn't turn up for our meeting yesterday. You must have tried reaching me on my phone as well. But Son, I am far off to reach you now. My journey as your friend was till this point only as I want to say goodbye to you.

Now, you won't need my presence around from now onward, the principles that I tried teaching you, will continue to be with you forever. No one can be with one forever, but the knowledge and experience will last long.

Now, you must be wondering where I must have gone that I am not going to come back. Son, I am not on this planet anymore and had just come to help you get out of the problem and to share my knowledge and experience with you. Now, my job is done and so I had to return. But, please don't be upset or sad about this. You must continue what you are doing and improve yourself with the knowledge and experience you get along the way.

Before signing off, I want to share my story with you. In my initial days, I was a worker in a small factory. During the strike, I got laid off from the job. So, I started selling things on the streets. Things were not so good, and I was just able to manage my home. Since I was doing everything myself, I was busy working all the time. I was so busy that I couldn't get time to talk to my son also. I wanted him to become a successful businessperson. In his final exams, he failed. He thought everything is over now. He was so depressed that he committed suicide. I couldn't save my son. I couldn't say to him that I wanted him to be successful and a good person and passing or failing in the exams cannot determine that. That time, I decided that I won't let this happen to any young person. I kept learning and practicing business principles and build many businesses. I too kept helping many such young people to come out of the problems. I educated them that 'failure in the exam is not an end, life is much bigger than an exam. So, when I saw that you were upset with your failure and life, I came to help you. And trust me, I will come over and over when I will see such young people.

Before ending the letter, I want to ask for a favor from you. I want you to help such young people while you are around.

Make this the purpose of your life and you will feel more successful than you feel by doing any other thing. God bless you, my son!

Bye, Bye!!!

Your friend,

Hari

Sam was crying as he folded the letter and put it back in the envelope. His entire journey of 'Failure to Success' flashed through his mind. He could clearly remember that evening when he failed in his exams and his first meeting with Hari and then every evening and every meeting he had with his mentor, everything. He was able to see, how Hari was happy when Sam completed his first task. Sam remembered Hari's lessons, the principles he taught, and most importantly, the way he taught. Sam decided that he would fulfill Hari's request and would help such kids who have failed in the exams and have given up.

'Health Hub' launch

Although Sam was in deep grief, he decided to start working on his venture because that's what Hari wanted him to do. Sam got back to work and started working with Sia and Raj After all the preparations they launched the 'Health Hub' in a big space on the outskirts of the city. At the entrance, there was a reception desk to greet customers. It had small consulting booths, seminar room, yoga and meditation room., new product counters, counters for their own products as well as for other providers as well. Overall, it was a dream setup for Sameer. He had kept a big photo of Hari at the reception and in his own cabin to remind him of all the life lessons he learned from his friend.

Sameer and the team had invited all their existing customers for the launch of this hub. All the visitors received some free products as a token of appreciation for their support. Sam, Sia, and Raj were personally greeting all the customers. Sia was explaining various subscription and membership plans to them. Raj was talking to their current partners and explaining to them about the new partnership model for the Hub and what are the offers for their existing partners. Sam was talking to various vendors whom they have allied with to provide products and services. It was overall a pleasant experience for everyone.

Sam's parents were also present. As soon as they enter the main gate, they saw the big photo of Hari and they were in tears. They remembered that evening when 'Sam met Hari', and remembered each evening when Sam returned learning something new from Hari. And today they were witnessing this evening. They couldn't believe the transition their son had due to this man. But unfortunately, they couldn't meet and thank Hari in person, so they paid their respect to Hari by lighting a lamp in front of his photo. Sam too was in tears to see all this. He was determined to continue the path shown by his friend, philosopher, and mentor, Hari.

Years passed and Sam continued expanding his businesses and starting new businesses. But at the same time, he did not forget his commitment and kept helping young people to help them rise from their failures. He had started an organization, to help students who have failed in their exams. He would mentor them personally the way he was mentored. Since he built the organization, he was able to reach many such students than he could have done it himself. Here too, Sam followed the principles of leverage, network to serve more such young people', that he learned from Hari.

I am sure, YOU too would like to join Sam in this mission. Don't you?

Summary

As we saw, we are born to live a free and happy Life. But unfortunately, we have grown up with lots of misbeliefs that limit us to live a mediocre life with financial worries. And, as you know that, if we continue to do what we are doing, we continue to get what we are getting. So, in order to get a better life, we must think differently and act differently. We need to unlearn some of the things that we have learned earlier to change our life for better.

The first step to get a better life is to 'Do what we love'. Our working life is almost 50% of our total lifespan and if don't do the things we are passionate about; we are living a meaningless life. As we saw that our soul is always in search for happiness, so, if we do what we love then, we perform beyond our abilities and that gives a sense of fulfillment and certainly a better life.

But, working on 'What we love' alone, won't be enough to live on this 'Commercial' planet. We need to earn a living to buy things we need, things we desire, to travel around the world etc. But again, just living the entire life chasing money without a good health and peace of mind won't give that life satisfaction. So, the second step is to understand, what exactly the money is, and try to find ways to create money by adding value and not simply to chase it blindly.

If you follow these 2 steps, your life will be 'worry free', and that will be the true life worth living. Isn't it? Afterall, it's your life, so it's you, to design it, no one else will.

Are you ready to unlearn, learn and design a better life for yourself? I wish you a great success in your journey of, **'Your Life, Your Way'.**

Thank you for reading the book. I hope you like it and you are ready to implement the principles mentioned. I would love to know your feedback.

So, please post your review and rating on the Amazon site.

Note:

We conduct separate workshops for the students who have failed in their exams and want to start something on their own. We help them build a career based on their passion and the 5 principles mentioned in this book.

...To know more, please call **+91 88799 75958**

or email to yourbigleap@gmail.com

YouNeur

We conduct separate mentoring programs for 'Young Entrepreneurs' who wish to start their own ventures'.

...To know more, please contact on +91 88799 75958 or email to yourbigleap@gmail.com

---

Personal Branding Workshop

We also conduct separate programs for 'Young graduates', for how to create a personal brand and grow quickly on the job ladder.

...To know more, please contact on +91 88799 75958 or email to yourbigleap@gmail.com

List of priceless Books

- ✓ Rich Dad Poor Dad (by Robert Kiyosaki)
- ✓ Cashflow Quadrant (by Robert Kiyosaki)
- ✓ Retire Young Retire Rich (by Robert Kiyosaki)
- ✓ Built to Last (by Jim Collins)
- ✓ Start Small Finish Big (by Fred Deluca-Subway)
- ✓ Grinding it Out (by Ray Kroc-McDonalds)
- ✓ Pour your heart into it (by Howard Schultz- Starbucks)
- ✓ You can Win (by Shiv Khera)
- ✓ Think and Grow Rich (by Napolian Hill)
- ✓ The Magic of Thinking Big (by David J. Schwartz)
- ✓ E-Myth (by Michael Gerber)
- ✓ Emotional Intelligence (by Daniel Goleman)
- ✓ 7 Habits of Highly Effective People (by Stephen Covey)
- ✓ Winning (by Jack Welch-GE)

My other books in the 'Money-Minds' series

	Passion to Success
https://www.amazon.in/dp/B089632ST4	
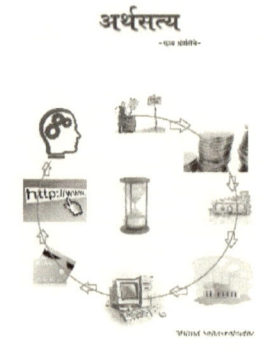	Artha Satya
https://store.pothi.com/book/ebook-milind-sahasrabudhe-artha-satya	
	Uncommonly Common
https://store.pothi.com/book/ebook-milind-sahasrabudhe-uncommonly-common	

www.ingramcontent.com/pod-product-compliance
Lightning Source LLC
Chambersburg PA
CBHW030817180526
45163CB00003B/1324